The United States and The United Nations

Books on Foreign Affairs from

The Johns Hopkins University
School of Advanced International Studies

Southeast Asia in the Coming World, Philip W. Thayer, ed.
The Threat of Soviet Imperialism, C. Grove Haines, ed.
Africa Today, C. Grove Haines, ed.
Nationalism and Progress in Free Asia, Philip W. Thayer, ed.
Tensions in the Middle East, Philip W. Thayer, ed.
War and Peace in the Law of Islam, Majid Khadduri
European Integration, C. Grove Haines, ed.
Alliance Policy in the Cold War, Arnold Wolfers, ed.
Islamic Jurisprudence: Shāfi'ī's *Risāla,* Trans. and with an Introduction by Majid Khadduri
The United States and the United Nations, Francis O. Wilcox and H. Field Haviland, Jr., eds.

The United States and the United Nations

Edited by
FRANCIS O. WILCOX
AND
H. FIELD HAVILAND, JR.

The Johns Hopkins Press, Baltimore 18, Maryland

These papers were prepared in connection with a conference on the United States and the United Nations under the joint sponsorship of the Johns Hopkins School of Advanced International Studies and the Brookings Institution.

JOSEPH E. JOHNSON
PAUL G. HOFFMAN
LINCOLN P. BLOOMFIELD
ERNEST A. GROSS
INIS L. CLAUDE, JR.
HARLAN CLEVELAND
FRANCIS O. WILCOX

Distributed in Great Britain by Oxford University Press, London
Manufactured in the United States of America
Library of Congress Catalog Card Number 61-16652

FOREWORD

RECENT WORLD DEVELOPMENTS, especially those related to the Sino-Soviet bloc and the new emerging states of Asia and Africa, have posed peculiarly difficult problems for the United States regarding its relationship with the United Nations. Some observers conclude that the United Nations has lost much of its usefulness as an instrument for dealing with certain critical problems, largely because of the increased influence of the Communist and underdeveloped countries within the organization. Others are less pessimistic but recognize that the United Nations faces severe tests in the coming years.

As a new administration in Washington began to grapple with these problems in 1961, The Johns Hopkins University School of Advanced International Studies and the Brookings Institution inquired whether the new Assistant Secretary of State for International Organization Affairs, Harlan Cleveland, would find it useful to meet with a group of people especially interested in and knowledgeable about the United Nations for a frank, off-the-record exchange of views on current and future United States policy regarding the United Nations. The response was favorable, and the two sponsoring institutions proceeded to plan such a conference in consultation with Mr. Cleveland and his colleagues as well as others outside the Department of State.

It was decided to focus the discussion on six major subjects, through six papers prepared by experienced specialists. Forty-five individuals participated in the conference, which was held at the Brookings Institution on May 12 and 13, 1961. Following the meetings, the papers were revised by the authors and are published here, with an additional paper written by Francis O. Wilcox, Dean of the Johns Hopkins School of Advanced International Studies and former Assistant Secretary of State for International Organization Affairs.

Others who attended the conference are: Hamilton Fish Armstrong, Council on Foreign Relations; Robert E. Asher, Brookings Institution; Stephen K. Bailey, Syracuse University; Jonathan B. Bingham, United States Representative on the Trusteeship Council; John Campbell, Council on Foreign Relations; William I. Cargo, Department of State; Benjamin V. Cohen, former Counsellor, Department of State; George C. Denney, Jr., Senate Foreign Relations Committee Staff; Clark M. Eichelberger, American Association for the United Nations; Dante B. Fascell, United States House of Representatives; Richard N. Gardner, Department of State; Benjamin Gerig, Department of State; Robert W. Hartley, Brookings Institution; H. Field Haviland, Jr., Brookings Institution; Louis Henkin, University of Pennsylvania; Arthur N. Holcombe, Commission to Study the Organization of Peace; John B. Howard, Ford Foundation; Elmore Jackson, Quaker Program at the United Nations; Gerard J. Mangone, Syracuse University; Carl Marcy, Senate Foreign Relations Committee Staff; Charles B. Marshall, Washington Center of Foreign Policy Research, School of Advanced International Studies; Leonard C. Meeker, Department of State; Forrest D. Murden, Standard Oil of New Jersey; Charles P. Noyes, United States Mission to the United Nations;

Norman J. Padelford, Massachusetts Institute of Technology; Morehead Patterson, American Machine and Foundry Company; Lucian W. Pye, Massachusetts Institute of Technology; Clinton Rehling, United Nations Special Fund; Eric Stein, University of Michigan; Kenneth W. Thompson, The Rockefeller Foundation; Marietta Tree, United States Mission to the United Nations; Richard W. Van Wagenen, American University; James J. Wadsworth, Peace Research Institute; Woodruff Wallner, Department of State; Albert A. C. Westphal, House Foreign Affairs Committee Staff; Virginia C. Westfall, Department of State; Arnold Wolfers, Washington Center of Foreign Policy Research, School of Advanced International Studies; and Charles W. Yost, United States Mission to the United Nations.

The general satisfaction with the conference can be attributed primarily to the wisdom and diligence of the authors of the papers, the skill of the chairmen who presided over the several sessions, and the constructive contributions of the other participants. Special thanks are due to the following staff members who managed the inevitable torrent of detailed arrangements with efficiency and equanimity: Harriet Daum, Patricia Martin, and Sandy Winne. The costs of the conference were shared by the two sponsoring institutions. The views expressed in the papers are those of the authors and do not necessarily reflect those of the other participants or the trustees, officers, or other staff members of the sponsoring institutions.

Francis O. Wilcox, Dean
School of Advanced International Studies
The Johns Hopkins University

H. Field Haviland, Jr., Director
Foreign Policy Studies
The Brookings Institution

CONTENTS

The United States and The United Nations

1

HELPING TO BUILD NEW STATES

by

JOSEPH E. JOHNSON*

IF THE PRESENT and foreseeable membership and activities of the United Nations tell us anything, it is that the central concerns of that Organization will reflect increasingly the central concerns of the new states. And the concerns of the new states do not involve, as a matter of primary interest, the achievement of international order and stability. They involve, rather, the substantiation of national independence and the assertion of the international power to which the new states feel entitled by virtue of their numbers. This is for us at once a problem and an opportunity: to build, with the new states, a constructive, dignified relationship that will work to both our advantages. What follows are some of my present thoughts on this problem and this opportunity. I offer them in the hope that they will stim-

* The author is grateful to Miss Patricia Wohlgemuth for assistance in the preparation of this paper.

ulate others to consider whether there may not be more ways than we have yet tried to approach the now familiar question of the new states.

The leaders of the new states, with a few exceptions, seem to know how they must proceed in building their nations. And they have made it abundantly clear that they intend—quite rightly—to take charge of their own destinies. To quote President Nkrumah's famous phrase: "We prefer self-government with danger to servitude in tranquillity." At the same time, many of us, from new states as well as old, look to the United Nations for help in minimizing the serious risks involved.

We Americans, again rightly, have understood that we have a stake in the building of the new states, though I am not sure we have always thought realistically about what that stake is. We have gone through the cycles of wanting friendship and pro-Western sympathy from the new states; now the talk is more of seeking their respect. This is a healthy change, but as we speak of respect we will do well to bear in mind the words of Franklin D. Roosevelt: "In the field of world policy, I would dedicate this nation to the policy of the good neighbor—the neighbor who resolutely respects himself and, because he does so, respects the rights of others. . . ." Such a policy will help promote the self-respect of all nations, which is the only sound basis for relationships in the pluralistic world of today. The comments of Edmund Stillman and William Pfaff in their stimulating book, *The New Politics,* are relevant here; they call for a United States policy whose object would be:

> to accelerate and influence a political process already under way—the rise of independent states, the diffusion of world power. This would be to promote the stability of international political relationships and

to re-create conditions in which professional diplomacy could function—diplomacy, that is, with all its uncertainties and its demands on nerve and intelligence, but diplomacy no longer reduced to futility by the very poverty of choices open to it. (p. 169)

With relation to the new states, this means participating—inside and outside the United Nations, and always out of self-interest—in the process of constructing confident, viable nations. For that purpose, I am convinced that we must accept the order of priority of the new states themselves.

The New States' Priorities

Briefly, if I understand them rightly, the priorities are these:

First, a state must be established. There must be a recognizable political entity with control over its own internal and external affairs. The establishment of such an entity may be facilitated by many things, singly or in combination—by religious or ethnic solidarity, by administration as a single unit over a long period of time, by a long common history, by geographical cohesion, and most especially by joint struggle against a foreign ruler. But many of today's states have entered the world distinguished, if anything, by a lack of strong national feeling on the part of their people and sometimes even of their leaders. The important thing has been the creation of an independent state. The age of "tutelage" is past, and, if truth be faced, we of the West who believed ourselves qualified to teach made very little use of the opportunity while we had it. But the leaders of the new states, as do many others, agree that political independencc is only a first step toward "real" independence.

The second step, the second priority, is that the state must be unified. Its people must begin to transfer their primary loyalty from the family, the tribe, the village, or the language group to the nation. It might be supposed that simple cooperation in national development could do the trick, but I can think of no examples offhand, and I suspect that the long, complex work of development does not generate the necessary emotional pull for the job of unification. Sometimes a prestigeful leader, a Nehru or a Nasser or an Nkrumah, may provide the unifying symbol. Sometimes it will be the rediscovery and glorification of past heroes or myths. More often the welding iron will be irridentism or fear of a common enemy or, most of all, and especially in Africa, suspicion, suspicion that the former rulers plan by devious means to retain their old control. Almost always unification involves strong central government, and a testing to see how far independence can be pushed.

Third, and only third, the new state must be modernized. To the leadership of most of these states this has meant primarily economic and social development. To some it has also meant a growing popular participation in the political process, although rarely along the lines of Western democracy. To virtually all it has meant a search—partly eclectic, partly creative—for institutional forms that will be peculiarly suited to the "personality" of the nation.

I do not mean to imply that establishment, unification, and modernization are exclusive stages each of which must be completed before the next can begin. In point of fact, most of the new states are attempting to do all or most of these things at the same time. But when choices must be made, I believe they are made according to these priorities. Burma's rejection of United States aid funds from 1953 to 1957 is perhaps a good example of the primacy of nationalistic needs (in this case, Burma's need to express tangibly its anger over presumed United States support for the activities of Nationalist Chinese troops in its northern provinces) over development needs.

In sticking to this order of priority, particularly in not placing economic development first, I believe the leaders of the new states show considerable political wisdom. After all, we have seen time and again that economic development does not produce either stability or popular government in, say, a colonial Congo or a feudal Iraq.

Establishment

What role can the United Nations play in these processes (assuming, as I shall, that the Organization does not founder on the rock of Soviet obstructionism)? It cannot take the lead, certainly; only the new states themselves can do that. But it can make a significant contribution. On balance, it is in the interest of the United States to further this effort, although we should recognize that there will be times, many times, when the interests of the United Nations, an organization devoted more and more to the needs and wishes of the small states, will not be identical with ours.

The United Nations has already played an important role in the establishment of new states, if only in fostering a climate in which retention of colonies is no longer fashionable. The stream of resolutions emanating from the General Assembly has focused attention on the crucial issues, and the growing bloc of new states has used its bargaining power well to force an ever faster pace of decolonization. The existence of the Trusteeship system and the reporting procedures under Article 73 (e) of the United Nations Charter have contributed by bringing the process under international scrutiny and by encouraging political, economic, and social development in these territories. I should not want to claim too much for the United Nations, but I suspect it is no accident that the Trust Territories, though more backward, have become established states more quickly than most of tropical Africa; that Togo was a bellwether for all of French African political progress; that Tanganyika will be the first major British-administered territory in East Africa to become independent.

On occasion, United Nations organs have taken a more direct part in the establishment of new states. Perhaps the outstanding example was the case of Indonesia, where conciliatory bodies created by the Security Council undoubtedly helped speed that country's separation from the Netherlands. In the case of Israel, subsequent recriminations aside, international acceptance of an independent Jewish state stems directly from a General Assembly resolution recommending partition of Palestine. And while the General Assembly could not even pass a resolution concerning Algeria until last year, I believe that the annual Assembly debates have given a vital international recognition and "legitimacy" to the National Front of Liberation, without which Franco-Algerian negotiations would be even further off.

The emergence of new states based on great nationalist movements is nearing its end, however, and for this reason I am inclined to feel that the various attempts at the Fifteenth General Assembly to establish a blanket target date for the independence of all non-self-governing territories are largely irrelevant. Each case inevitably differs somewhat and should be considered separately. The British East and Central African territories are clearly on the road to independence, and there seems little inclination toward unwonted delay on the part of the United Kingdom government. The situation in Algeria has at last begun to move off dead center. Even Spain is beginning to respond to international pressure with respect to its overseas territories. The Union of South Africa is a special problem, similar to yet different from colonial questions. Perhaps only in the case of the Portuguese territories could a target date put significant new pressure on a recalcitrant colonial power, although one suspects that the problem of persuading Portugal to change its policies must be tackled largely outside the United Nations and primarily by that country's traditional allies.

When it comes to the remaining dependent territories, most of them small and many not viable as individual nations, a one-colony-one-state pattern is less likely to be appropriate, although continued colonial status is equally unacceptable. Article 73 of the United Nations Charter, relating to non-self-governing territories, speaks of "a full measure of self-government" rather than of independence. The Fifteenth General Assembly noted that the former term included "free association" or "integration" with an independent state as well as emergence as a sovereign entity. (Resolution 1541.) In relation to integration and association, the establishment of future new states may offer opportunities for the United Nations to play more than a hortatory role. I am encouraged by the recent case of the British Cameroons, in which, in my view, the United Nations conducted itself with admirable maturity. Assembly debates produced a consensus that the two parts of the Territory did not constitute a viable entity and that each would have to choose to join either of its two neighbors. The presence of United Nations observers at the plebiscite ensured the legitimacy of the outcome and enabled the world community to withstand the pressure of those who wished to reopen the question. It is to be hoped that the United Nations will play a comparably responsible role in Ruanda-Urundi, the next problem of this sort.

What should be the future of New Guinea, complicated as it is by Indonesia's claim to West Irian? What about the Pacific Islands? Note that Western Samoa is scheduled for independence at the end of 1961. Is there not room for some creative thinking as to the future of the various island chains? The General Assembly, influenced as it is by new states, will surely give increasing attention to the status and development of these islands. Perhaps the archipelago countries—the Philippines, the West Indies, even Indonesia—will have some wisdom to contribute out of their own experience. Perhaps the already overburdened Secretariat can find time for still another task: assessing the elements that will be relevant to a smooth transition.

There may be cases—some island groups, for instance, or small territories like Hong Kong—where neither full independence nor amalgamation with a new or existing independent state proves appropriate. Such areas, according to one suggestion, might be given associate membership in the United Nations, similar to that used in the regional commissions today. Such a status would enable residents to communicate directly with the world, in dignity, without having to take up the full burdens of independence. The task of working out details of this "leftover" problem might be turned over, in the first instance, to a combined Trusteeship Council and Committee on Information from Non-Self-Governing Territories, both of which are beginning to run out of business, or to some successor body.

We Americans are prone to forget that the United States has

a special problem in the Trusteeship field and may find itself the last "colonial" power on the Trusteeship Council. Within the next two or three years all the Trust Territories save our 97-island "strategic" Trust in the Western Pacific (and Nauru, which will in any event be uninhabitable by the year 2000) will have become independent or otherwise disposed of. Although we are presumably protected from adverse resolutions in the Security Council by our veto there, it is inconceivable that we should escape pressure to give up these islands. Now is surely not too early to begin considering what we plan to do about them. Emil Sady once suggested federation with Guam and incorporation as a United States Commonwealth.[1]

The United States must also find ways to convince the new states that we really mean—as I believe we do—our anti-colonial protestations. This is as much a matter of style as it is of voting, but it is voting, too, and we must remember that completing the process of liberation is the first order of international business for most of the new states. Parenthetically, we must try to find another word for Soviet "colonialism"; it should be clear by now that we will never get the ex-colonies to see the satellites in the same light, even though many sincerely disapprove of Hungary, Tibet, and similar cases.

Unification

Once a new state is established, what then? The role the United Nations can play at this stage is exceedingly delicate but exceedingly crucial, particularly now, when most of the states recently admitted to membership are preoccupied with problems of unification and of asserting their independence.

[1] *The United Nations and Dependent Peoples* (Washington, D. C.: Brookings, 1956).

We can already see that, while the picture is still fairly fluid, there will be what one might call "adjustment disputes" over borders, property rights, and similar problems. This is particularly true in Africa. Mauritania is a good example; the Somali-Ethiopia border dispute is another. It seems to me wasteful and exacerbating to have all these disputes automatically blown up to the proportion of major international issues in the General Assembly or Security Council. I wonder whether it might not be useful to explore the possibilities of settlement at the regional level, with procedures tied more closely to the United Nations than those of the Organization of American States, and with disputes passed on to the full Organization only if necessary. Use might also be made of standing conciliation procedures. Although the recommendations of the Interim Committee of the General Assembly on mechanisms for peaceful settlement came to little in the late 1940s, and although they were based largely on inter-war European experience, it might be worthwhile to take another look at them in the light of present circumstances. Might it be wise, for instance, to revive the idea of a panel of potential members of commissions of enquiry and conciliation? Is it also worth studying traditional non-European methods of peaceful settlement to see which can be adapted in a United Nations context? One way or another the United Nations has a clear duty and a reasonable potential for easing this period of the new states' transition to unity.

We of the older states must realize that the problem of unification is something different from economic and social development and different from establishing "law and order." If we fail to understand this, and if United Nations decisions do not reflect that understanding, the new states may well be tempted to acquiesce in the destruction of the Organization itself. This is one of the great lessons of the Congo experience. Many of us failed to realize that the African states could not admit the possibility of Katangan secession, could not even support United Nations negotiations with Katanga as a quasi-independent state; to have done so would have been to have encouraged by implication every divisive tendency in their own countries. It seems to me that this accounts for the stand of a number of countries including Ghana and Morocco.

It accounts in part, too, for the disrepute into which the concept of federation has fallen in many of the new states. Federation too easily becomes confederation or, even worse, Balkanization. Many people in the United States have tended to believe our brand of federalism can and should be easily transferred to the new states. But these states have regional problems that we never faced. It is certainly true that many of them must take political account of recognizable sub-regions in their governmental structures and are eager to know what others have done. But I suggest that a more suitable channel for advice on this subject is the United Nations, where the experience of members like India, Canada, Brazil, and Yugoslavia, as well as the United States, can be drawn on and where Secretariat advisers would have less emotional commitment to a specific governmental form. Private individuals of high reputation, working under the aegis of the United Nations, might be used with special advantage.

The important thing is that the new states develop their own locally rooted forms of government. As Herbert Spiro has pointed out,

> The most successful parts of the [American] Constitution—its federal aspects, the Supreme Court, the amending procedure, the Presi-

dency—were not copied from models in the Old World, but created by inventive genius that applied itself to solving the new problems of the New World.[2]

The new states are already embarking on an equivalent path. India, for instance, can be called a one-party democracy, which some would consider a contradiction in terms. The Guinean Democratic Party, which wholly controls that country's government, is a monolithic structure with an active mass membership; this is not democracy as we know it, but neither is it Soviet-type Communism. In Pakistan, where parliamentary government failed utterly, we have an example of military rule with burgeoning institutions of "basic democracy" at the village level. Forms of government like these begin to reflect the new needs of the new states, each in its own particular way. More than material advances, the development of popularly suggested indigenous institutions is our best insurance that the new states will remain independent and will resist the temptation to adopt that other major Western system, Marxism-Leninism.

It might be well to give greater attention to programs of helping new states enhance and glorify their cultural heritage in the eyes of their own people, for much the same reason. I am thinking of money to print good vernacular literature and to translate it into other local languages, tape recorders for catching provincial folk music, support for national art and music collections, as well as scholarly research, archeology, and international recognition through cultural festivals or cultural-exchange missions. Such programs help promote a sense of national identity quite as much as they promote mutual under-

[2] "New Constitutional Forms in Africa," *World Politics* (October, 1960).

standing. It is my impression that neither the United Nations Educational, Scientific and Cultural Organization, nor any other similar agency, has yet shown the inclination to make a major contribution in this field. The United States Government and private foundations can also do more along these lines.

We must be prepared for the emergence in the new states of rather more centralized governments than we would choose for ourselves. But that does not mean we should close our eyes to infractions of human rights, including the right of public dissent. On the contrary, we should take greater advantage than ever of the United Nations setting to make known our concern for, and "to promote . . . observance of, human rights and fundamental freedoms for all. . . ." This obligation of the Charter rests as heavily on all other members as it does on us. Just as we must endeavor to clean our own house, so we should expect them to. While we must try to understand their special problems, we would be less than American if we did not encourage where possible an enlargement of the area of individual freedom.

But we must at the same time remember that we are dealing with states with an almost pathological fear of "neo-colonialism," of losing the substance of independence and retaining only the shell. The United Nations is one large testing ground of the sincerity of the former colonial powers. I do not mean to imply that we will, or should, agree with the new states on all questions. Many of their basic interests in one way or another coincide with ours—political independence, economic development, and social advances—but others do not. There will be sharp differences over the speed of change, the role of gradualism, private investment, military alliances, and similar problems. More important than votes in this connection is style, evidence that the older states respect the newer ones' need for dignity and self-confidence. Memories of colonial injustice and humiliation have made the leaders of the new states extremely sensitive to condescension, to political arm-twisting, and to being taken for granted. The fact that they know they need much of what the older states have to offer in the job of modernization only compounds that sensitivity.

We have too often neglected this matter of style in small ways as well as big, in keeping up informal day-to-day contacts as well as in seeking—and taking—small states' advice on questions of special concern to them. Although the example does not come from the United Nations, I would point to the Assistance Group of the Organization for Economic Cooperation and Development as an example of a good intention which may fail for not yet having recognized the need to make the recipient nations a part of the program from the very beginning. Basically, perhaps, what I am saying is that we must make it clear that we know, first, that the ability of a nation's representatives and the integrity of its policies do not depend on its age or the size of its budget and, second, that any nation is ultimately the judge of its own best interests.

The framework of a universal organization, in which nations participate as of right, not sufferance, can help to mitigate these problems and to allow for such adjustments of differences as are possible. For the West particularly, there is much to gain from sincere and tactful use of the United Nations in this way. Being the objects of greatest suspicion, we stand to reap the most from proof that the suspicions are invalid. We of all people should find the United Nations a congenial forum, since the ideals expressed in its Charter and the institutions established under it stem directly from our concepts of democracy.

Modernization

The United Nations system has already proven its value to the new states as a platform for airing their views. It must still prove its value as an effective instrument in the next stage—modernization.

Of course a beginning in this direction has been made, though on a much lower level in terms of money and influence than many would like. The following gains may be counted. At the insistence of the new states, the importance of social as well as economic development has been recognized and incorporated into the planning of UN programs. The fluctuation of raw material prices is being seen as a priority problem. A considerable amount of technical assistance experience has been amassed. The importance of capital to go along with technical assistance is increasingly realized, and, again under pressure from the new states, the Special Fund and the International Development Association have been established. The World Bank has, in its limited field, proved itself with extraordinary effectiveness. The statistical research and analysis gap is narrowing slowly, thanks to some excellent studies by the Secretariat, the World Bank, and the regional commissions. But past experience has done little more than suggest the potential role of the United Nations and related agencies.

I agree with Assistant Secretary of State Harlan Cleveland that "the development of the United Nations operational capability should now be a central target of American foreign policy."[3] But we must acknowledge that the United Nations is

[3] Address before the American Society of International Law, 29 April 1961.

not now in a position, administratively, to absorb much new responsibility. Such major operations as the early United Nations Emergency Force in the Middle East and the present United Nations Operation in the Congo have been hastily-put-together affairs which have made exorbitant demands on Secretariat facilities and have caused the rest of its work to suffer. The financial problem is, of course, of the utmost importance. In the development field, reorganization is already overdue, as Andrew Shonfield admirably shows in his recent book, *The Attack on World Poverty*. The specialized agencies have become competing empires rather than parts of a rational whole. The World Bank is not set up to meet the capital needs of really underdeveloped countries, and the foreseeable resources of the International Development Authority are inadequate.

The regional commissions are still almost untapped organs. Now that their majorities are firmly indigenous and well organized, they could become nuclei for action as well as discussion, for channelling advice and even material, and for multiplying the effectiveness of the trained Africans and Asians who are in such short supply. The Economic Commission for Latin America has already shown that a dynamic staff can be the key element in the working out of common market arrangements. The Economic Commission for Asia and the Far East has contributed much to the planning of the Mekong River project. The commissions have been eager to play a more central role in the development process. Sub-regional offices such as are now contemplated by the Economic Commission for Africa could provide permanent, readily available sources of advice to governments. Short-term seminars might be used to acquaint higher government officials with continent-wide problems and resources. Some regional economic and even political matters might be administered directly by the commissions. But the commissions have been greatly hampered by the marked coolness displayed toward them by the West, which has preferred ECOSOC, presumably because it has greater relative power there. Similar comments can be made regarding the new Committee on Industrialization. The time has come to reconsider our attitude and policy. I would go further and urge experimentation to see how much responsibility the regional commissions are willing and able to take on.

In sum then, the first and most urgent task is to see how the United Nations' administrative resources can be enlarged and redirected. This will be a major job, for it will require the agreement not only of 99 governments but of a multitude of jealous bureaucracies within the United Nations constellation. The civilian operation in the Congo, which is doing an amazing and much overlooked job, is not really a good example of what might be done, since its work is in the nature of an emergency holding operation; nevertheless, the activities of the 200-odd man team in the Congo do prove that, under pressure, the various parts of the bureaucratic puzzle can be brought together to operate with some semblance of unified direction.

Assuming administrative capability, the United Nations could make a significant contribution to the modernization efforts of the new states. In certain circumstances, consideration might even be given to putting the United Nations in a position to administer large, multi-national programs—for example, the Mekong River project—directly, under appropriate accountability to the General Assembly or to the Economic and Social Council, and to the countries involved. Arrangements concerning retention of sovereign rights, allocation of revenues, and related problems would be difficult to work out, but where riparian states are clearly unable to mount a major project themselves, these obstacles might not prove surmountable.

For the most part, however, the United Nations will function as a supplier of advisory and operating personnel, and money. Although the subject of financing is outside the scope of this paper, it is important to note that major new development capital will have to be found and provision made for adequate participation of receiving countries in its allocation.

To help meet the lower level personnel needs of the new states, an International Peace Corps could greatly enlarge the supply of semi-professionals, and I am glad to see that President Kennedy is already pushing this idea in connection with the creation of our own national Peace Corps. On a higher level, the existing United Nations Program for the Provision of Operational, Executive and Administrative Personnel as the Servants of Governments (OPEX) is only the beginning of what could be a world-wide manhunt for skilled professional personnel ready to fill jobs wherever needed, possibly on a semi-career basis. I should underline "only the beginning," however. In the first two years, while still in the experimental stage, OPEX made some twenty-six appointments. This year—with Assembly agreement that it shall be a continuing program and with a budget of $850,000—OPEX will be able to make between 80 and 100 additional appointments. This is clearly the proverbial drop in the bucket. OPEX has already had over 200 requests for personnel this year.

When it comes to the highest administrative levels, the problems are two-fold: first, to add to the total numbers available, and, second, to raise the competence and selfconfidence of those already holding responsible positions. Whether many new states will want to seek outside assistance at this most sensitive of levels is an open question. But it seems to me that only a universal organization such as the United Nations can think of supplying personnel at this level, and I am not sure that any but long-term international civil servants would begin to be acceptable. I do not know precisely how much has been done in the way of seconding Secretariat personnel for special administrative jobs, but it seems to me that this device might be utilized to a much greater extent.

The other side of the coin would be to post officials from the new states to the Secretariats of various United Nations organs for fairly extended periods, possibly as long as a year, although it is admittedly difficult for the new states to spare them. This would have the merit of exposing them to presumably advanced administrative techniques and the equal merit of permitting greater participation by the new states in the day-to-day work of the United Nations. I realize that this scheme, if carried out on a large scale, may raise questions for the development of an international civil service, but I believe the gains might outweigh the losses.

Integration

All that I have said so far assumes that the independent nation-state is the goal, the desirable end-product. And clearly this *is* the first priority from the new states' point of view. Since the end of World War II, however, we have become aware that ever greater interdependence is more appropriate to our times in terms both of economic development and of international stability.

It seems to me important that trans-national economic and political links be encouraged in the new states as well as in the old, particularly in Africa, which is so full of small states of doubtful viability. The recent history of Africa does not offer much ground for expecting political integration, the optimism of some Africans and Americans notwithstanding. The most recent example of disintegration is the failure of the Mali Federation. The Federation of Rhodesia and Nyasaland will almost surely break up; Ruanda-Urundi and the Congo remain question marks. Nevertheless, one should not overlook such experiments as the Pan-African Freedom Movement for East and Central Africa, the Ghana-Guinea-Mali Union, the cooperative arrangements of the Brazzaville twelve, the Casablanca five, the Maghreb secretariat, and the apparently successful union of the former British and Italian Somalilands. The initiative for an integrative scheme, functional or political, should surely come from the countries concerned if it is to have the best chance to succeed. But equally, the attitude and response of the outside world, particularly where technical arrangements need to be worked out, can help or hinder the growth of international ties.

It is regrettable, therefore, that along with historical and other factors tending to foster separatism, United Nations practices, generally speaking, tend to encourage an emphasis on the single independent state, both by giving representatives of the new states a forum from which they can speak directly to the world and by the constitutional provision giving each state one vote; the importance of the latter has even been enhanced by the development of bloc voting.

If, as I believe is the case, the development of larger groupings should be encouraged rather than discouraged, thought needs to be given to procedures that might at least begin such a development. I wonder what the implications would be of a suggestion that, for example, Benelux or the Ghana-Guinea-Mali Union be permitted to send one delegation to the General Assembly without having to accept only one vote. Could we not envisage working toward revision of voting procedures—and perhaps other steps—that would place a premium on functional or political integration, at least in relation to those bodies where a specific joint arrangement is applicable? For instance, in the non-political field, could the integration of airlines, in the pattern of the Scandinavian Air Lines System, be encouraged by providing a more important role in the International Civil Aviation Organization for countries that do integrate than for those that do not? I recognize that in encouraging larger groupings one would have to avoid falling into the rigid tripartite pattern now advocated by Mr. Khrushchev. But clearly it is important to raise the issue in order to stimulate thought on the subject.

Mutual Accommodation

It has often been said that one of the most valuable functions of the United Nations is to integrate the new states into the world community. This is, in my opinion, true. Participation in the daily work of the Assembly and the various commissions and committees quickly creates a network of shared interests, shared experiences. The special caucuses, such as those held by the African-Asian group, and the Commonwealth group, are particularly effective in helping new states to develop a coherent foreign policy. And the need to vote on a variety of issues compels governments to consider the implications of international issues from the point of view of their own over-all interests. Several individuals whose judgment I respect and who have had the opportunity to observe the performance of the new states in the United Nations much more closely than I, are convinced that on balance their participation has encouraged responsible consideration of foreign policy issues rather than irresponsible meddling. These persons have also remarked upon the great speed with which representatives of the new states have adjusted themselves to the new environment.

It is true that the spokesmen for the new states—like the rest of us—tend to put their positions more firmly and often more radically in public debate than they do in private. After all, the General Assembly is more of a propaganda forum than a parliament. One lesson to be drawn from this by the United States, in the interests of moderation and mutual accommodation, is certainly to engage in more advance informal consultation and negotiation with all interested parties. Another is to curb our propensity for assigning labels like "pro-Communist" and "undemocratic" too quickly.

But we of the West, and perhaps Americans above all, need to recognize that integration into the world community does not mean that the new states will—or should—behave like us or that responsible consideration will necessarily bring results to our liking. We do ourselves a disservice and are doomed to disappointment if we automatically assume that failure of the new states to accept or even to understand our point of view stems from political immaturity or irresponsibility, and that, given time, they will accept our canons of behavior. The process of integration requires mutual adjustment.

Indeed, I wonder whether the greatest contribution of the

United Nations will not be, ultimately, to smooth *our* adjustment to the fact of the new states, to help *us* accommodate ourselves to a world that is changing rapidly and will change even more drastically in the future.

An immediate, practical problem of accommodation is, of course, the enlargement of the membership of the Economic and Social Council and the Security Council, on which the new states are, as all agree, inadequately represented. I tend to sympathize with the new states' feeling that they are being made to suffer unfairly for United States and Soviet intransigence over the issue of Chinese representation, with the consequent Soviet refusal to consider revision of the United Nations Charter. Our attempt to blame the problem on the Soviets is not really a satisfactory response, since the majority of the new states believe our China policy is mistaken. Can we not try to find a positive proposal that would, at least on an interim basis, begin to meet the problem? For instance, can we agree to invite one or two representatives, to be chosen by the African-Asian caucus, to all Security Council debates as a regular practice regardless of whether or not their interests are specifically involved? If the Congo debates are any sign, something of this sort may be happening willy-nilly. Would associate membership of ECOSOC, with voting privileges, require Charter revision? Some students of the Charter think not. Surely this does not exhaust the list of possibilities. In addition, greater importance for the subsidiary organs of ECOSOC would help mitigate the frustration of the new states at their minimal representation on the over-all body. I have already commented on the need to increase participation of the new states in the work of the Secretariat. These suggestions are made not only to take account of the legitimate demands of the new states, but also to point up the need to give the new states a greater stake in the preservation of an effective United Nations in the face of Soviet attacks.

These mechanical adjustments are relatively simple. Much more difficult will be the less tangible but nonetheless necessary adjustments in mental attitudes that will have to take place. These words from a recent issue of *The Economist,*[4] although they were written with reference to the Commonwealth, seem to me particularly apposite:

> The kaleidescope has at last rearranged itself into the design dictated by the arithmetic of the contemporary world. The great black and brown nations like India, Pakistan and Nigeria have moved decisively closer to the centre of gravity. It is the small white nations, like Australia, New Zealand and Canada—whose combined population is less than that of Nigeria—that are now seen clinging to the spokes of the pattern, moving when the hub moves, blown by the winds of change.... It is clear that this upheaval will require matching upheavals in the mental attitude of everyone concerned....

Reinhold Niebuhr once observed that old elites always suspect new ones of being immature, childlike. We have for too long told ourselves how much we had to teach. We must begin to tell ourselves that we also have much to learn.

[4] March 25, 1961, p. 1160.

2

THE SIX IMPERATIVES OF ECONOMIC AND SOCIAL PROGRESS

by

PAUL G. HOFFMAN

Two-thirds of the world's people, two billion of our fellow human beings, are dreadfully poor. Hundreds of millions of them are in active revolt against the continued acceptance of their poverty, illiteracy, chronic ill health and early death. They now know that a better life is possible for them and their children, and they are determined to have it.

Not only they, but people in the advanced countries too are awakening to the most pervasive and explosive idea of this Twentieth Century—that body-destroying and soul-destroying poverty can be wiped off the face of the earth, and must be. This idea is electrifying the world, sharpening the focus of human aspirations, providing a catalyst in local and international affairs more potent than the cold war or the atom, and presenting modern statesmen with their greatest challenge.

Today, with good cause, the speeding of economic and social progress in the low-income countries is a dominant problem for *all* countries, one intimately related to the national purpose of each country and determining its own security and economic health.

But accelerating development is not simply a question of increasing substantially and rapidly the output of goods and services in the low-income countries, desperately important as that is. The crucial issue is that this be done in such a way that the spiritual and intellectual as well as material needs of men are satisfied.

If dangerously rising tensions are to be channeled to serve mankind instead of bring about its destruction, the people of the north and south and east and west must join together in a cause as common to them as their destiny has become. This they are longing to do: people everywhere are eager to use their energies for constructive purposes.

What then do the masses of all countries seek? (1) to live without war; (2) to enhance the dignity and worth of the human person through respect for the equal rights of all men and women and of nations large and small; (3) to establish conditions under which justice and respect for the obligations arising from international agreements and international law can be maintained; and (4) to achieve social progress and better standards of life for all in larger freedom.

These noble supranational ideals are taken from the United Nations Charter. They have been formally subscribed to by ninety-nine nations, who have also undertaken to employ national and international machinery to accomplish these aims. Democratic international instruments for promoting their achievement exist in the organs and agencies of the United Nations. And it is my thesis that these nearly universal instruments should be used to the maximum, that is, much more fully than they have thus far been used.

I intend to limit my observations to problems of economic and social development and possibilities for hastening their solution. However, I would first stress that the ultimate purpose of the foreign policy of every nation should be to construct in this interdependent world a workable international order—an order which fosters the maximum of freedom and expanding human welfare compatible with peace and justice. Clearly this requires universal institutions—political, economic and social—with purposes, principles and procedures that have been broadly agreed, are respected in practice and strengthened with experience. None of these institutions can flourish in isolation; weaknesses in one will sap the vigor of the others, and success in any will support progress in all. Therefore, the foreign policy of every nation should be an ensemble of coherent measures designed both to improve the climate for fruitful cooperation among all peoples and to reinforce the instruments indispensable to peace and progress.

Dimensions of the Challenge

Perhaps nowhere are the opportunities and rewards for strengthening international cooperation so promising as in the vital field of economic and social development. Here is a task truly of, by and for the world, one that should rally all nations. The nature of this task, however, must be clearly understood; only then can suitable means for accomplishing it be formulated, only then can the role that the United Nations could and should play be appreciated.

The job of speeding economic and social progress is one of

challenging dimensions. There are some 100 important countries and territories associated with the United Nations which by any measure must be considered economically underdeveloped. Over one billion three hundred million pitifully poor people now live in those countries. (There are some 700 million additional people in economically underdeveloped countries not associated with the United Nations, including mainland China, North Korea and North Viet-Nam.) And in a short 35 years, barring a major war or other unforeseen development, the population of these low-income countries will have doubled. This raises to a new power the urgency for rapid, adequate action.

The task is also one of bewildering complexity. Involved are economic, political, religious, legal, educational and social factors, as well as psychological elements including taboos, mores and too often quite incomprehensible attitudes of peoples and their governments. To add to the difficulties, the situation—physical and human—in no two low-income countries is exactly similar. Indeed, there usually are also immense differences among the various regions within a developing country. Therefore the programme of economic development for each of the 100 countries must be hand-tailored to meet its own multi-facet needs and possibilities, while taking account as well of those of other nations in the world community.

The issue before us is far from purely technical, or even economic. Nor is it one of achieving marginal changes. What is required is a nearly total transformation of society, national and international.

In the underdeveloped part of the world new and viable nations must be forged, and political emancipation must be accompanied by social and cultural emancipation, if significant technical and economic development and improved living standards are to be achieved. Honest, efficient and forward-looking governments will be required, with leaders capable of bringing about fundamental reforms and supporting imaginative, responsible policies—for the sense and reality of social justice and a feeling of shared sacrifice, purpose and hope among the people are essential to the environment in which development becomes possible.

In our advanced countries basic changes are also required. Old modes of thought and concentration on narrow goals will not suffice in the last half of this century as they seemed to do in the 1950's. We need to develop a 360° perspective and adjust our values, our energies to the realities of the wide world become a neighborhood. This involves for us changes of heart and habit running the gamut from integration and high levels of employment at home to creating a new, dynamic international public policy.

There are many hopeful signs that leaders in the low-income countries are gearing themselves for their immense tasks, that policy makers, opinion makers and the people in the industrialized countries are facing up to their challenge to greatness, and that the countries of the world are increasingly disposed to undertake together the hard thinking and hard work their common problems impose. These are encouraging facts, for it is on the battlefront of human purpose that the major fight must be won in the struggle for improved well-being, greater freedom and international order.

Prospects for Better Progress

If the nations singly and jointly apply themselves to the job with vigor and imagination, there is no reason why an undreamed of rate of progress cannot be achieved.

In the first place, nearly all of the one hundred low-income countries and territories associated with the United Nations have in their physical and human resources the potential means for achieving decent standards of living for their people. The problem is to get those resources into production multiplying today's output of goods and services.

The second reason for cautious optimism is that modern technology has provided ways to expand productivity enormously. Not the least of these tools is that of building-in, through investment in organized research and development work, the leaven for sustained economic growth.

The third factor offering some promise of reasonable progress is that we have over recent years developed machinery, national and international, specifically designed to facilitate economic and social advance. These institutions, though often very rudimentary, are vehicles for rethinking ways that society can help fulfill human needs, and are instruments for inducing desired change, e.g. through the judicious application of knowledge and capital, manpower and goods, to make economies more efficient. Organizationally, too, we are not starting from scratch.

Even so, the progress of peoples will be uneven; the most we can hope for is that by the end of this decade, say ten or fifteen or more key low-income countries will have made the most of the opportunities offered, planned and built wisely, put forth the necessary domestic effort, attracted a large amount of outside assistance, and achieved real breakthrough toward self-propelling, self-generating economies with relatively substantial increases in living standards. Others, with less favorable circumstances or not willing to make the necessary effort, may have attained less than the average income increase. And still others may have retrogressed. But those that did break through would give heart to the others—and perhaps an example. We must hope that the examples will show that appreciable strides can be made without tyranny and with a minimum of social cost.

How can we hasten the building of that healthy world economy which is the prerequisite for healthy democracies and international stability? How can we best assist a dozen or so countries to reach take-off in the 1960's, and others to get underway in the '70's and in the '80's?

We have learned from experience what impedes progress toward those objectives, and what is imperative to accelerate the development strides of emerging nations. The 1950's have spotlighted, amongst other things, the limitations of outside assistance, and also the strategic functions it can perform.

Earlier I observed (1) that the resources for substantial improvements in living standards are present in nearly all low-income countries; (2) that modern technology provides improved methods for raising production and productivity; and (3) that new national and international institutions offer exceptional means for a more efficient organization of progress. Now let us take a closer look at these points.

The Pre-investment Imperatives

Each day at the United Nations brings me new evidence that the low-income countries are richer in promising physical resources than anyone has thought. But the rate of revealing the potentialities of these countries' soil, water and forests has been and remains woefully slow. Even with international aid, the systematic study of natural resources, for what they could do to increase the wealth and well-being of the people in those countries, has barely begun.

Our priorities were wrong; we understood rightly that large investments were required, but we neglected to face the fact that money will not venture into the unknown, and that it will, on the other hand, voluntarily come forth when opportunities for its useful and profitable investment are demonstrated. Millions of dollars for resource surveys can get billions of dollars to work.

Thus we arrive at our first imperative for speeding economic and social development. It is that the people of the low-income countries and of the advanced countries as well should immediately increase several-fold the relatively small sums of money and supply of talent and equipment required to find out what the natural resources of the low-income countries furnish to work with, and to demonstrate the technical and economic feasibility of investments to get those resources producing.

The human resources of the low-income countries have been even more tragically neglected than their physical resources. While the development of natural resources is relatively easy with modern methods, the development of the human resources is much more time-consuming and costly. Yet, investment in human beings is the most promising investment of all, as experience in highly industrialized countries, including Japan and the Soviet Union, and in certain less-developed countries, has made crystal clear. People with requisite knowledge and skills are the prime movers in the development process. And all peoples have the capacity to learn, to become good administrators, good managers, doctors, scientists, engineers, teachers, technicians, extension workers and craftsmen.

But, here also the local and international effort has been too little and too late, reflecting a colossal failure to understand the critical importance of developing *within the low-income countries* teachers and facilities to educate and train *local* people to make effective use of their resources. Thus we are today faced with the staggering task of training millions of people for high-level and middle-level functions in transforming stagnant economies into dynamic economies, and of training tens of millions for skilled occupations. Beyond this is the need to educate as rapidly as possible hundreds of millions in primary schools, secondary schools and adult education programs. Modern society and government require citizens who can read and write, think and behave rationally and become voluntarily diligent and disciplined contributors to the progress of their country and the world.

So our second development imperative is this: to multiply many, many times the local and international resources presently available to develop in the low-income countries the human capital required for a more satisfactory and safe rate of economic and social advance. Even if this is done, the funds available will be far from sufficient to satisfy all needs. Part of them should therefore be used to define balanced educational programmes fully geared and periodically adjusted to meet the manpower requirements of national development plans. In most countries these programmes will include a considerable expansion in the training of secondary school teachers.

Knowledge and Capital for Development

Another promising and grossly under-utilized lever to raise living standards is modern science. There are no imaginable limits to what the findings and methods of science might bring if they were more fully applied to the problems of development. New sources of energy, salt water converted into fresh water, new crops adjusted to unfriendly soils, better and cheaper products from traditional and invented materials, new tools, new processes, new thoughts—the possibilities are breathtaking. However, except in medicine, this handmaid of man has hardly deigned to glance at mankind's most urgent needs; the minds and the motives in the social as well as the physical sciences are but rarely oriented towards the underdeveloped world. Yet victory here could be infinitely more important than conquests, for instance, of outer-space.

Here then is our third imperative: more of our resources must go into research on the techniques and means of accelerating development in the low-income countries. This is at present largely a responsibility of the industrialized countries, although many of the investigations must be carried on in the field and others ought to be, so as to train local people in the use of this versatile instrument that could add cumulative new factors to development formulae and make the picture of our future radically brighter.

Our next imperative need is to strengthen greatly the capacities of the national programming and planning services in the low-income countries. The allocation of local and outside resources for development cannot be made intelligently if there is not a plan with realistic priorities for balanced economic and social growth. Such plans not only provide a reasonable framework for public investment; usually they also furnish guides to development trends which are welcomed by private investors.

All of the imperatives we have thus far considered come under the heading of pre-investment activities. Together they add up to a new industry with relatively low costs and high returns—the business of creating actual opportunities for investment of domestic or foreign, public or private capital. My United Nations colleague Hans Singer puts it this way: "These activities provide the infrastructure for investment, build the *capacity* to create wealth." They thus should have a high priority in international assistance programs, and be supported particularly by those who fear that even the ability of most low-income countries to absorb aid is threateningly limited.

The fifth imperative we face is in the field of investment itself. I have suggested earlier that there are not likely to be special difficulties in obtaining directly productive capital when conditions are demonstrated to be right to make such investment feasible, effective and rewarding. But this is not the case when outside resources are required for non-revenue-producing facilities such as roads, ports, water supplies, schools or hospitals and public health services.

Such installations and services have an important place in any programme for development, and themselves usually constitute pre-requisites for revenue-producing investment. Yet investment in them can only be paid back over a long period and out of the general increase in the level of economic activity which they have helped engender. Therefore, new sources of finance and new conditions of repayment have had to be established—that is, long-term international public loans with very nominal or no charges for interest and with repayment installments not beginning for a decade or so. But obviously in the not too distant future the sums available for loans of these kinds will have to be increased substantially; they promise exceptional returns.

The United Nations and Development Assistance

And now we come to the final imperative I would propose to intensify effective development action. It is this: for compelling practical, psychological and political reasons, a greater proportion of international public assistance—in pre-investment and investment fields—should be channeled through the United Nations.

Let me stress that I do not believe for a moment that all or even a major part of international aid should be administered by the United Nations. There will be many occasions when a country might well, for one reason or another, prefer to use direct bilateral channels, or regional agencies not integral parts of the United Nations system. In some cases there may be sound technical as well as political justification for this.

The approach to aid should be pragmatic rather than dogmatic. In selecting the modalities of aid for economic development, this involves taking into account two key questions. The first is how to make every dollar of international assistance produce the greatest returns in economic development. The second question is: how can this aid be channeled so that it not only produces maximum economic impact but also intensifies the experience of multilateral cooperation and strengthens the institutions of world order? These are very pertinent questions, for *the resources for economic development are too small to be wasted, and any opportunity for building international solidarity is too precious to be missed.*

My personal belief is that candid consideration of these factors will lead governments to call upon the United Nations to administer a steadily greater proportion of the increasing development assistance they must and will provide in their national interest. They can turn to the United Nations with full confidence, for a remarkable phenomenon has occurred over the past fifteen years. It is the steady growth of the United Nations into an operational instrument capable of responding with ever greater efficiency and flexibility to the complex needs of its Member States.

Public attention in this period has been focussed on debates whose vehemence alone demonstrates the need for them, and on the beneficial effects of United Nations political and peace observation work, for instance, in the Middle East and the Congo. Some may even know of such amazing organizational achievements as the United Nation's clearing of the Suez Canal, and doing so speedily and at a fraction of the cost that was expected, or know of the good work of United Nations civilian operations in the Congo to meet emergency relief requirements and carry on the arduous task of rehabilitating the public services and economy of that country which is almost as large as continental Western Europe.

If the blue helmets and emergency measures have captured the public eye, what has almost completely escaped its notice is the vast amount of other and quieter but no less indispensable work accomplished under the blue flag of the United Nations.

This is especially true of the United Nations' wide range of study and action to promote economic and social advance in scores of low-income countries and territories in Latin America, Africa, the Middle East and Asia. There has been a thriving growth in these activities in recent years—as insights have led to ideas and ideas have led to action programmes of both immediate and long-term significance.

It would, of course, be impossible, in an article of this length, to describe even sketchily the multitudinous deliberative and operational activities performed by the United Nations and its related agencies to aid low-income countries.[1] I should like, however, to indicate certain developments and considerations arising from them which merit attention in determining the future orientation of assistance programmes.

Salient Developments in U.N. Aid

Thus, it is worthy of note that since 1957 the annual resources available to the United Nations for technical and pre-investment assistance have grown three-fold, and that this has permitted not only an expansion of earlier worthwhile activities but also a new dimension in the effort to meet development imperative earlier mentioned.

Under the United Nations family technical assistance programmes alone more than 3,000 experts are working this year in nearly 100 low-income countries and territories to apply their

[1] Among sources for detailed information are The Brookings Institution's "The United Nations and the Promotion of the General Welfare," U.N. Document E/3347 —"Appraisal of the Scope, Trend and Costs of the Programmes of the United Nations, Specialized Agencies and the IAEA in the Economic, Social and Human Rights Fields," and in annual and other reports of United Nations organs and affiliated agencies.

experience to the removal of bottlenecks to economic and social progress. They come from 70 countries and territories, many of these, like India and the United Arab Republic, themselves recipients of United Nations assistance. Also under these programmes, some 3,000 technicians and officials from low-income countries are being given advanced training abroad in more than 80 countries during 1961. These figures represent substantial increases in the advisory and training services of the United Nations and the specialized agencies in public administration, health, education and manpower, food and agriculture, industrialization, transport and communications, meteorology, social welfare and many other fields. A larger proportion of this assistance is now going to the newly independent countries.

Also of particular importance to these countries is the threefold expansion in resources for the United Nations to send to requesting governments not just advisors but personnel to occupy senior operational and executive positions and become full officials of the governments to whom they are provided. As in the case of most United Nations technical assistance experts, one of the duties of these officers is to train local counter-part personnel to take over their responsibilities.

A major step forward was taken by the United Nations when it created the United Nations Special Fund. This grew out of the deepening appreciation of the fundamental role that relatively large pre-investment projects could play in accelerating economic growth. One of the principal aims of the Special Fund in providing assistance is to create in the low-income countries conditions that will make investment feasible and more effective. For allocation in 1959, 1960 and 1961, Governments of 78 countries, rich and poor, volunteered contributions totaling the equivalent of $112 million. On the basis of these and anticipated pledges, the Special Fund has approved 157 projects whose average duration is between three and four years. Their total cost will be roughly $305 million, with the Special Fund granting $131 million and the recipient Governments supplying the remaining $174 million.

The projects are of highest priority in the developing countries concerned, and are designed to meet critical needs for knowledge of the potentialities of the physical resources of the low-income countries, for developing latent human resources through technical education and training, and for learning through applied research ways to produce the vastly larger quantities of food, housing, goods and services which people in those countries require to make their lives more productive and satisfying. Admitting the present underdeveloped nature of the statistical background and projection techniques, a carefully reasoned estimate of investment potential generated by the level of Special Fund assistance approved in 1959 and 1960 is a yearly rate in the near future of over $2 billion of domestic and external capital. The Special Fund's carefully selected pre-investment assistance should not only help to attract new capital to worthy development activities; it should also ensure that scarce investment funds are not wasted because of inadequate preparatory investigation.

This assistance will give a new and needed impetus in other directions as well as in that of finance, notably by strengthening the capacities of the people and the institutions in the low-income countries, and by its insistence that the government of the countries in which the projects are to be implemented make a substantial contribution to their cost and assume a very large measure of responsibility for their success.

Thus the Special Fund hopes to respect a crucial fact of economic development. It is that the major responsibility for achieving economic and social progress in a country rests squarely upon the government and people of that country. Outside aid can help, but only in cases where there are dedicated leaders and the people are making a maximum effort to help themselves.

On the investment front, too, the resources of United Nations agencies have grown and the range of activity has widened in essential directions. The creation of the International Development Association, affiliated with the World Bank, is an important response to the need, stressed during many years in the United Nations, for loans on easier terms and conditions than the commercial standards of the World Bank.

The International Development Association (IDA) now has over 45 signatories, and subscriptions totaling $900 million. It has under investigation projects ranging from irrigation works to industrial plants, many of them in countries at very early stages of development. Terms of financing are to be flexible and bear less heavily on the balance of payments of borrowers than the terms of conventional loans. With IDA's management and staff the same as those of the Bank, one may be confident that IDA will apply the same high standards in project preparation and execution as does the Bank. All must welcome this promising new agency for international investment and wish its growth in the future.

These and other developments in the scope of United Nations family assistance have challenged the organs and agencies involved to integrate their concepts and operations in order to use their limited funds to meet really urgent needs of the governments and countries. Some of the newer programmes have joined with older ones in sharing administrative facilities and thereby lowering costs; examples of these include the Special Fund and the Technical Assistance Board on the one hand, and the World Bank and IDA on the other. The Special Fund has called upon the United Nations and many of the Specialized Agencies for expert assistance in evaluating project requests and, in the case of every project thus far approved, has been able to designate the United Nations or one of these agencies as Executing Agency for the projects.

Not only have the daily contacts between these bodies multiplied, but programmes of concerted action have also been developed. At the same time coordination is being steadily intensified in the field as country programming and longer term project commitments are undertaken. The United Nations Regional Economic Commissions are bringing more of their growing knowledge to the service of operating programmes and are also using and assisting the joint Resident Representatives of the Technical Assistance Board and the Special Fund in the increasing number of less developed countries where these Representatives are being stationed.

The assignment to the Resident Representative of important responsibilities on behalf of the Special Fund has enhanced his position both *vis-à-vis* the Executing Agencies of large Special Fund-assisted projects and *vis-à-vis* the government which can depend upon his firm but friendly counsel. Other factors as well have enlarged the functions and raised the status of the Resident Representatives and their staff, thereby greatly extending the services they can render the governments to which they are assigned. All of this is also bringing United Nations assistance agencies closer together as a team in the field, and gearing their programmes for maximum impact in stimulating balanced economic and social advance.

Potentialities of the U.N.

The broadening of the role of the United Nations in development is not a fortuitous accident; rather, it represents a practical response to the necessity, in our contemporary world, of adjusting individual efforts to global requirements. Powerful economic as well as political forces are at work to bring about a growing integration of the world community, and the United Nations and its related agencies are uniquely fitted to assist in the task. There are many reasons for this. Here are some of them:

First, because, as I earlier recalled, the developmental problem is a world-wide problem; it is therefore a problem which requires the brains, the resources and the cooperative efforts of all countries. In the words of Secretary-General Hammarskjold, the United Nations "remains the only universal agency in which countries with widely differing political institutions and at different stages of economic development may exchange views, share their problems and experiences, probe each others' reactions to policies of mutual interest, and initiate collective action."

Second, in the United Nations and its fourteen specialized agencies reposes the richest experience that can be found anywhere in virtually every field of developmental activity.

Third, the United Nations draws on the whole world for its technicians.

Fourth, assistance through the United Nations guarantees that paternalism does not stunt the effect of aid; United Nations assistance is a completely cooperative endeavour with a voice given to countries whatever their size or wealth and with all countries contributing to the cost.

Fifth, because the low-income countries know that United Nations assistance programmes are financed by more than eighty countries, both rich and poor, it is possible for the United Nations to insist that the recipient countries put forth a maximum of self-help.

Sixth, and most significant of all, the United Nations, the principal world-wide partnership of equals, is also the instrument for peaceful change which is preferred by virtually all of its ninety-nine Member Nations.

Areas of Need for Further U.N. Action

The United Nations *is* uniquely endowed to assist in achieving an expanding world economy with generous benefits for all. What are some of the many specific areas where the United Nations could provide additional leadership and help avoid the waste of unrelated initiatives and conflicting policies?

One such field is that of expanding world markets, particularly for the exports of low-income countries.

Another area of need for cooperative action is that of stabilizing commodity markets; it makes no sense at all for the industrialized countries to give economic aid and then, as recently happened, deny them export earnings in almost exactly the same amount because of the fall in world prices for the commodities they export.

New joint measures could also encourage a greater flow of private capital from the advanced to the less developed countries.

Concerted study and initiatives in the United Nations might also bring about a dramatically important programme to use, for development purposes, not only food surpluses, but obsolescent and excess equipment and unused industrial capacity in the developed countries as well.

Through a rationally organized process of consultations, the United Nations could, better than any other agency, play an increasingly useful role both in the harmonization of national economic policies and in the formulation of international economic and social objectives.

Dramatic possibilities exist for employing United Nations machinery to attract and concentrate bilateral and multilateral assistance on projects of unusual importance. This U.N. "umbrella" function's usefulness has been demonstrated in the United Nations' Lower Mekong Basin Project and in the IBRD's Indus River Scheme. It could be extended, for instance, to other areas and other fields; education in Africa is but one of these.

United Nations agencies should be supplied steadily increasing resources for international public investment in development, including, in due course, a substantial enlargement in IDA's financing capacity.

A most immediate need is to increase the funds for the United Nations Expanded Programme of Technical Assistance and the Special Fund to the $150 million target agreed by the U.N. General Assembly. This sum for the year 1962 is only slightly more than it cost to clean the streets of New York City over the past 12 months! Surely the governments of the world can find it possible to reach this target for these programmes in the year ahead. It would be easy for them, if they were willing, to invest much more in this vital technical and pre-investment assistance to help create the conditions for world prosperity, for peace and freedom, and, by using the United Nations, to strengthen the institutions of our nascent international community.

The need is urgent and the time is ripe for major new initiatives. A leading representative of an underdeveloped country only a short time ago expressed what is in the minds of many people around the world: "Under President Roosevelt, the United States took the lead in creating the United Nations and related institutions such as the World Bank. Under President Truman, it co-sponsored the creation of the U.N. Expanded Programme of Technical Assistance. Under President Eisenhower it proposed the establishment of the United Nations Special Fund and the International Development Association. What can we expect of the United States in major initiatives under President Kennedy?"

3

THE NEW DIPLOMACY IN THE UNITED NATIONS

by

LINCOLN P. BLOOMFIELD

RARELY IN ITS sixteen-year history have such dire and portentous things been said about the United Nations. Our friends in the press have always enjoyed the role of Cassandra. But suddenly they have a lot of company. Only a few times in the past has there been such profound contrast between the standard expressions of hope and confidence in the United Nations and forebodings about the time of troubles it is facing—and the United States along with it. There were only a few times, but it is useful to remember that there were such times. It would not hurt to lengthen our historical view sufficiently to recall at least three other periods in the United Nations' short history when the odds all at once seemed to lengthen and all but a few chronic—or professional—optimists joined the chorus of gloom.

One such time of trouble was the first big "Morning After."

1946 was a downward slide into disillusionment, and by mid-1947 the scales had, by and large, dropped off a good many starry eyes—including my own. The attendant political pain was intense. Another time of trouble was the unnerving period during the first half of 1950. It began with the communist countries progressively boycotting the United Nations, and it culminated in a war. There followed a period in which, among other things, the Soviet Union did its best to make an "unperson," in the Orwellian sense, of the Secretary General of the United Nations. For what historical consolation it brings, their unilateral liquidation of Mr. Lie was even more comprehensive than that of Mr. Hammarskjold, at least so far.

The third time of trouble was a more subtle one, and the present is perhaps most intelligibly seen as an extension of it. For by the close of the 1955 General Assembly attentive observers were discerning clear signs of the end of American hegemony and the beginning of a new political configuration in the organization. Stalin had been dead for two years, the Bandung Conference had given shape in and out of the United Nations to the interests of 29 nations, and mutual nuclear deterrence was going to be the preferred shape of strategic planning on both sides. Indeed, five years ago the United States Government was holding elaborate post-mortems on the general subject of "How can American leadership in the United Nations be restored?" As of 1955 it was fair to say that nothing would ever be quite the same again.

I have indulged in this backward look not because I underrate the new problems—far from it—but because they are not all precisely new. Their roots go deep into the past, and, as always, the past has something to teach about the present and the future. This awareness is not necessarily reassuring. But it does mean that we are not entitled to act too surprised and shocked by the more recent unfolding of international political patterns that seem to show up so vividly in the United Nations. It also means that some of the more blatant nonsense that is now being said about the United Nations has been said before, and with just as little attention to fact and reality.

But having said that, certainly there is a staggering agenda of problems facing American diplomacy in the United Nations. The problem, as always, exists on all levels from the pinnacle of broad national strategy to the trenches and redoubts where tactics win or lose the battle. What is happening in the United Nations is a problem not only for the diplomat on the ground and on the home desk but also for the planner and strategist who has only too infrequently succeeded in integrating the United Nations sector with the rest of the national policy pattern.

Out of the multiple problems in this realm, two areas of prime concern stand out: first, the almost tropical growth in political and parliamentary influence of the Afro-Asian states; and second, the campaign by the Soviet bloc to reform the United Nations in the Communist image.

The Impact of the New Membership

It has always been true that the United Nations diplomatic scene makes sense only when it is explicitly related to events and forces external to the organization itself. This is the familiar argument, immortalized by Sir Gladwyn Jebb, that the United Nations is a mirror of the world around it and that if the reflection is ugly the organization should not be blamed. I profoundly believe this to be true. But against it there has always been the complaint by some of Sir Gladwyn's fellow Europeans that the ratio between the United Nations and the outside world is by no means a simple one-to-one correlation. This view, in its most critical form, has always castigated the United Nations as an inciter to riot. According to its doctrine the United Nations, because of its composition and because of its inherent ideological bias, distorts and magnifies to intolerable proportions certain matters of crucial interest, particularly in the colonial area. This arsonist argument has by no means prevailed in the United States or Scandinavia or in many other areas. It is far more commonly held that United Nations attention and pressure, particularly in colonial relationships, is not only right but can actually improve situations which, if uncontrolled, would produce even less acceptable results.

This issue is by no means a purely theoretical one. If it is true that the Afro-Asian group is using its near-majority position in the United Nations simply to stir up racial and political trouble in the Portugese colonies, and if one were confident Portugal would act with farsighted and enlightened preparations for self-government, then we should re-examine our own premises. The evidence is all to the contrary, and we can only conclude that while United Nations debates may encourage unrest, the conditions for unrest were there first. It may be that without the United Nations the colonial powers might have hung on a little longer in certain areas. But it is unlikely that the basic contours of the problem would be very different.

The revolutionary process that has taken place in the once-imperial world to the south has left a legacy of colossal problems about how the new nations are to be brought into a durable and mutually satisfying relationship with the established order as we know it. The categories of problems involved in the transition to nationhood are familiar ones and many of them are covered elsewhere in this book. But the political and diplomatic effects of the process are intimately tied to the substance of the problems. Most of all, the diplomatic task is bound up with the priorities assigned by the countries directly concerned, as they—not we—view those priorities.

The countries we are speaking of all share in varying degree the qualities of being non-European, non-white, politically neutralist, and anti-colonial. I have cited the colonial problem. Many people give equal weight to the problem of gross economic disparity between rich and poor nations. Until the gap begins to close, no enduring stability is possible between the nations involved, or in any diplomatic forum in which they interact. Unquestionably this issue is paramount, and American diplomacy in the United Nations has labored for many years to offset our negative attitudes toward multilateral financing of economic development, toward more predictable international commodity prices, and toward the problems of foreign and absentee ownership of resources. American policies in some of these areas are, I believe, loosening up.

I myself give equally high rank to the racial issue. If the behavioral sciences have anything to say about contemporary diplomacy it is undoubtedly in this realm of misunderstandings, attitudes and images, hostilities and frustrations. At root, George Kennan is right about the domestic basis for successful diplomacy. For so long as the United States tolerates racism at home, that long will all our bridges to the black, brown, and yellow nations be shaky and poorly supported against stress.

The north-south revolution by its very nature poses the problems of statehood itself—of evolving political forms, of relating the central governments to regions and integrating these nations in other ways. Perhaps most importantly, there are problems of dignity and of the pride which representatives of new nations have displayed abroad since the first American diplomatic agents refused to bend the knee to foreign potentates.

Clearly, if there were no United Nations these issues of both substance and diplomatic style would still be the vital stuff of international politics in much of the world. Because there is a United Nations, they come together there and in their totality add up to a new political force which by its numbers and by its pivotal role in the East-West competition confronts the Western powers with perhaps its central diplomatic challenge.

As a matter of fact, the United States has in past years occasionally found itself in a minority position on some issues, particularly when it came to such ideological assertions by the United Nations as the right of states to nationalize their resources. For there is today by no means the assurance of safe majorities, across the board, that we had in the 1940s, or even of the slim assurance of the 1950s when, on human rights covenants, Security Council elections, self-determination definitions, and financing economic development, we were far from having our own way.[1]

The New Arithmetic

The new arithmetic now comes into focus. The facts about it have become commonplace. From 10 at the San Francisco Conference, the Afro-Asian membership has grown to 46 and will

[1] See Lincoln P. Bloomfield, *The United Nations and U. S. Foreign Policy* (Boston: Little, Brown, 1960).

soon increase again. Where there were two African states south of the Sahara, there are now suddenly 20. Add Cuba, and, sometimes, Mexico, and it comes very close to a numerical majority. Add the Soviet bloc, grown from 5 to 9, plus Yugoslavia, and only 9 more are needed to make up the crucial and decisive two-thirds in the General Assembly. Another popular way to arrange the numbers is to add together all the underdeveloped countries, i.e. the Afro-Asian group plus, more or less, Latin America. Without the Soviet bloc this hypothetical majority already commands a two-thirds vote, and, with the Soviet bloc added, it has a clearly commanding position.

There have been no such exact combinations—yet. But these possible combinations of voting strength furnish the concrete basis for much of the concern about the future of the Western position in the United Nations. Actually, the numbers can be used to support any side of the argument. In the last General Assembly some votes tended to show that the worst had finally happened—if the worst is a minority position for the United States. The neutralist call for a summit meeting carried over United States opposition, 41 to 37. The American proposal on Arab refugee relief received only 31 votes to 30 against and 15 abstaining, the first time in memory that the United States had not carried its way on that issue to which we contribute the lion's share financially. Then we lost, 10 to 47, in the final refugee resolution with the unacceptable reference to property rights. The United States was in the minority in the vote on the Mexican proposal to discourage states from using their territories or resources to interfere in the Cuban civil war. It was in a tiny minority in a committee vote on a crucial paragraph on the Cuban resolution. And we could not carry a proposal to finance the Congo operation even though it cut the share of the poorest countries up to 75 per cent. The measure carried only after the reduction was made 80 per cent.

The same Assembly session, however, can demonstrate the opposite case. Who in a pluralistic world could legitimately ask for more decisive support than the United States received in such votes as these: 62 to 12 to reject Soviet disarmament propaganda moves in the plenary session; 54 to 10 to require orderly rather than spectacular debates on the RB-47 incident; 53 to 24 to seat the Kasavubu delegation from the Congo; 81 to 9 to approve the 1961 budget to which the communist bloc objected so vigorously; 61 to 27 for a proposal on Cuba that we could live with—far more, incidentally, than we had much right to expect under the circumstances; and 83 to 11 on a Congo resolution calling for effective measures by the Secretary General, in the midst of the Soviet attack upon him and on the office as presently constituted?

A third set of votes is interesting because of its ambiguity. Here one comes closer to the truth about the divergent interests within the Afro-Asian bloc and the growing fluidity in alignments in general, particularly the present distinction between "British" and "French" Africans, reinforcing the impression that the present may be a poor time for confident political prediction whether optimistic or pessimistic.

One of the interesting phenomena of the United Nations has been the superimposition of the political process upon that of diplomacy. The substance, that is to say, is diplomacy; but the milieu is that of politics, with qualities common to both Ward 6 and the Congress of Vienna. The growth of bloc politics in the United Nations was in this sense inevitable. What is now happening is a shift within the blocs themselves, a fluidity of voting alignment reflecting the dynamic shifts within regions such as Africa and Latin America. The Afro-Asian bloc, for example, has become four discernible sub-blocs: the five Casablanca powers, the French community nations, the pro-Western, and the middle of the road group.

Given this fissiparous trend, the Afro-Asians alone still do not hold the parliamentary whip-hand, even though East and West seek their support. In the 41 to 37 vote on their summit proposal the Communists were among the 17 abstainers. The Afro-Asian call for a United Nations referendum in Algeria received 40 votes in favor, 40 against—a striking example of the close balance between the forces involved. Time and again the bloc failed to get two-thirds or even a simple majority on such proposals as breaking relations with the Union of South Africa, giving priority to the Angola question, or adjourning debate on the Congo.

Of course the numbers tell only part of the story. The case for pessimism is incomplete without the slap administered to the United States by the Africans, through the Nigerian delegate, in the matter of the proposed American aid program for Africa. Opinions differ about this: was the American gesture insufficiently followed up by concrete proposals? Was the Nigerian delegate being excessively unkind to us for his own purposes? Or are all American initiatives, however sincere, to be unavailing until the storm has spent itself a good deal more? Here the armchair strategist can only fall into the traps of insufficient knowledge and Monday morning quarter-backing.

But once again the coin has two faces. It is widely believed that in the crucially important Security Council vote in the early hours of February 21 supporting the United Nations operation in the Congo and authorizing the use of force, if necessary, to prevent the occurrence of civil war, the Soviet Union shifted at virtually the last minute from expected opposition to abstention. The resolution was sponsored by three Afro-Asian states, and the episode dramatized the dilemma facing both the Soviets and ourselves. For both powers must constantly reappraise their diplomatic priorities, and each periodically has to balance its books in just such haste.

The private citizen can only applaud the important ways in which United States policy has recently improved its posture with respect to the new countries. The whole country stands in the debt of Ambassador Adlai Stevenson for so effectively sensing and acting upon American diplomacy's principal tactical deficiency in New York. But surely planners and headquarters policymakers should share credit for curing American policy of its most schizoid defect by planting our banner decisively on the side of racial equality and rapid independence. American support for United Nations inquiries into racial disorders in Angola had a remarkable effect, at least in the short-run, on neutralist opinion. In all fairness we should also recognize that an important threshold was crossed even earlier when in March, 1960, the United States agreed in the Security Council that South Africa's *apartheid* policy involved the maintenance of international peace and security and was a fit subject for Council action. Yet that action underscored the larger predicament for American United Nations diplomacy in terms of Western alliance policy.

The Problem for the Western Alliance

One of the grounds for the Western pessimism about the future of the United Nations stems from growing European irritation with the "irresponsible" majorities that ride roughshod in areas that are traditionally no one else's business. General de Gaulle's extraordinarily virulent attack on the United Nations seemed to put an exclamation point to increasing European disaffection. Some students of Western unity are saying that the United States must again face a choice between the Western alliance and the will-o'the-wisp of African and Asian nationalism. There are many today who will argue that the United Nations can only worsen Western relationships while holding no promise whatever of winning the ephemeral, unprofitable—even hopeless—popularity contest with the Soviets in—or out—of the United Nations.

This line of reasoning involves several dangerous fallacies. First of all, there is nothing new about the European problem in the United Nations. Some of our Western European allies distrusted and feared United Nations action, particularly on colonial matters, long before the newer nations developed their present political strength. Both before and after Suez, United Nations majorities have run against what some European nations conceived to be their vital interests as well as their right to privacy in colonial affairs. Without documenting the analysis (which I have made elsewhere), I believe that the final passing of the colonial issue in its present form will profoundly transform the European-United Nations relationship, just as it will transform European-African relations over-all. The truth of this is demonstrated by the shadings among Western Europeans on this issue discernible for some years past. The spectrum began with those having least sympathy with the United Nations and allegedly most to lose from its intervention in colonial matters—France, Portugal and Belgium, with the added French nostalgia for lost hegemony in League days. Mid-point was

Britain, where the parties were sharply divided on the United Nations-colonial issue, and Mr. Macmillan's winds of change had rather long since been measured and quietly but irrevocably yielded to. At the far end were countries such as the Netherlands—which but for the West New Guinea issue would have been planning and acting even more positively in the United Nations in such fields as economic development—and Italy, which looked across the Mediterranean in a frame of mind geared to an entirely new and clearly noncolonial era.

The end of the colonial era in Africa will not end the problems for Western diplomacy. It is predictable that they will still be numerous and thorny. But the sooner that day comes, the sooner the West, the United States, and the United Nations will be relieved of what has been a truly crippling incubus. One predictable consequence will be the acceleration of the integrative process within Europe. This in turn could make real the vision some Europeans already hold when they look to the future: a united Europe which once again can have a strong and constructive voice in the multilateral diplomatic forum.

From the standpoint of American strategy, another thing needs to be said about Western alliance problems in the United Nations. The end of the colonial problem in its present form will doubtless bring Western Europe and America closer together in their policies toward other parts of the world. There will be an appreciably greater community of interests around the globe than there is today. But until that happens we cannot assume that it is possible somehow to solve the problem of splits between America and its allies, in or out of the United Nations, by applying to all issues wherever they may arise the same coordinated strategic planning and thinking that properly underlies alliance programs in the North Atlantic area.

The NATO foreign ministers meeting at Oslo recently registered their determination to do just this. Surely closer consultations can only be salutary. But it does not alter the central principle involved. The *raison d'être* for NATO is a common interest in that area, an interest unquestionably shared by its members. But at least at the present time there is an acute divergence of interests elsewhere, a divergence that goes a great deal deeper than lack of consultation. Common interests in the North Atlantic area simply do not mean that interests are shared everywhere else. The French make very different estimates from ours about what is at stake in Southeast Asia; the British think us childish in our China policy, while we consider them naïve; the Belgians consider us unsympathetic in the Congo, and we deem them unrealistically nostalgic; and the Portugese believe us to be disloyal—as well as stupid—in Angola, while America reciprocates these sentiments in equal measure.

No single solution exists, in or out of the United Nations, to the task of knitting together the Western alliance. Diplomacy can lubricate the points of friction, and in the end the Atlantic community, in divesting itself of colonialism, will survive and flourish. But the task of foreign policy in the meantime is to manage a dual policy—alliance knitting as well as sustaining an independent American policy towards areas where we feel our policies to be correct. The task of United States diplomats is made no easier by this duality. But no one ever pretended that diplomacy was easy.

Possibilities and Limitations

How then, preferably with our European allies, if necessary without them, can we work through United Nations diplomacy to contain the energetic and even unmanageable forces of nationalism and social revolution sweeping across the globe and coming into high relief in the United Nations? The substantive answers lie beyond the scope of this paper. But the over-all prescription is not a new one. If an author can be pardoned for quoting himself, there is no reason to amend words written well over three years ago:

> The success of the West in gathering support from these countries has become increasingly dependent on the stands which Western nations take on issues of primary importance to the peoples of that "third world." These have not been such issues as capitalism vs. Communism, or German unification, or liberation of the satellites, but colonialism, "self-determination," economic development, and racial discrimination. Out of the present membership of [99] approximately [63] members for one reason or another see these as the crucial issues and put the United States to the test in regard to them with increasing frequency.[2]

That this was approvingly quoted in writing by Mr. Selwyn Lloyd indicates that we are far from alone in this insight. Undoubtedly the United States could better serve its own interests by taking more affirmative steps to relate itself to the United Nations majority. It can respond to the prime interests of that majority by sponsoring positive United Nations programs in

[2] "The UN and National Security," *Foreign Affairs* (July, 1958), p. 599 (figures updated).

the areas of financing economic development, technical assistance, human rights covenants, racial problems, and improved formulas for rapid yet cushioned independence. It has become almost a cliché to call for such policies. But at the same time there is danger in expecting too much of them.

For there is a special refractory quality to this problem which sometimes seems to render it impervious even to maximum efforts. The reason for this is that the problem *has* an inherently intractable quality to it. We may have the best will in the world—which I do not really doubt. We may even develop for the United Nations a more purposeful American strategy and detailed policies to back it up—and here we may still have some distance to go in our foreign policy capability. But even so armed, all kinds of disappointment and frustrations are bound to lie ahead. It is going to take a long time to eradicate the traces of resentment, hatred, envy, bitter memory, and hurt pride which almost without exception linger in the psyches of the new countries—more exactly, in their leaders. We must learn to live with this and to concentrate in the short term, the middle term, and the long term on the promotion of enduring relationships based on common interests, shared enterprises, and increasingly mature assumption of responsibilities. If we can win any popularity contests in the process, so much the better.

The danger for the majority of the new countries is not that they will go communist. It is that they will not go forward. To the extent that the United Nations can demonstrate its relevance to the central issues surrounding the process of modernization in responsible freedom, to that extent it can be a positive factor in American strategy during the difficult period ahead. I have in mind the extent to which the United Nations is a place to engage the new countries in common enterprises, to assist them in getting up momentum, to the extent that it supplies an educating sense of involvement in the management of international business, a revealing exposure to the problems of others, and a demonstration of the difference between the styles of free countries and police states, and above all to the extent that in our own domestic arrangements we set an example (and incidentally, learn to become properly hospitable).

To the extent we do none of these things, or do them badly, or half-heartedly, or fall into the ancient trap of letting tactics become the master of strategy instead of *vice versa,* to that extent our fears can be made to come true. To that extent the United Nations can be transformed into a genuine danger rather than what it is now, an opportunity to do some needful things, and a test of whether we are skillful enough to carry it off.

One of the foundation stones of American policy toward the new nations is that they need us—our know-how, our money, our ideology of freedom. But that is not the whole story. We need them quite as much, and we need them in and through the United Nations. The worse things become in the cold war, the more need there is going to be for countries that are not affiliated with either side. This is a compelling argument for keeping some of these countries truly neutral. Diplomatic planning requires the cultivation and availability of true neutrals who can play a multitude of roles in the peaceful settlement of disputes and in healing breaches of peace. I am well aware that this is precisely the contrary of the view being so vehemently advanced by the Soviet Union. This brings me to the other great constellation of issues—Soviet policy in the United Nations.

The New Soviet Offensive

It is becoming difficult to pick up a newspaper without reading an editorial alleging that the Soviet Union is seeking to destroy the United Nations. The Soviet onslaught of 1960–1961 has shaken us all. But perhaps it is not entirely accurate to say that the Russians have a present intention to smash the United Nations. If they had, they have only to leave the organization; predictably about a third of the membership would follow. Certainly the Soviet Union wishes to destroy the United Nations in the sense that, if it had its way—which it does not—it would undoubtedly wish to see eliminated not only the United Nations but SAC as well, just as it would prefer a communist takeover wherever it now has only a quarter-loaf. But the Soviet leaders are realists and pragmatists when it comes to adjusting priorities.

If they do not have a present intention of smashing the organization as they would and could by deserting it, one can then see how within the framework of temporary adjustment to reality they are doing better in the United Nations than ever before and may well estimate their prospects for political profit in and through the organization as increasingly promising. In this last session of the Assembly, according to one record keeper, the Soviets received the largest vote in history for a proposal they sponsored (29 in favor, with 53 in opposition on a proposal to convene the Congolese parliament within 21 days). Moreover, Moscow has shown a renewed interest in Secretariat positions. Soviet interest in filling its quota in the International Atomic Energy Agency considerably antedates the same interest in the United Nations. Most recently there has been reportedly noticeable improvement in the quality of the Soviet personnel detailed to Secretariat positions. The improving Soviet position in the United Nations suggests a more sophisticated explanation for recent Soviet moves to alter the structure of the office of Secretary General than the rather simple-minded one of blind destruction.

The present situation makes better sense when read against a broader backdrop. In essence the Soviet Union has now applied to the United Nations the same principles of power and organization that Moscow has applied to *all* international institutions in recent years. Beginning roughly with the flight of Sputnik I in October, 1957, Soviet leadership has made no secret of its revised assessment of the world equation of power and influence. The strategic reappraisal carried with it the policy consequence that diplomatic arrangements henceforth should reflect the new equation. From that time on, the Soviets have demanded "parity" in one international setting after another, and in several important instances prior to demanding that the United Nations oust Mr. Hammarskjold and convert the office of the Secretary General into a triumvirate representing the West, Communist bloc, and neutralists, and requiring unanimity for action.

The United Nations Ad Hoc Committee for Outer Space met for a year without the Soviet representative (and four others) because the composition negotiated in the fall of 1958 did not satisfy the Russians. And its successor Committee has made no headway because the principle—or rather, the successor principle—of recognizing Soviet leadership in the space field by making a Russian chairman of the proposed scientific conference has not been agreed to by the West. The deadlock on the composition of the United Nations Disarmament Committee was broken only by making it a committee of 99 members. Meanwhile the West had held its nose and actually agreed to the principle of parity at the Foreign Ministers meeting in the summer of 1959. Consequently the ten-nation Committee on disarmament that met in Geneva in the spring of 1960 (vainly as it turned out) reflected a formula of five and five—five members of the Communist bloc and five from the West—a far cry from the three-to-one and four-to-one negotiations among the foreign ministers since the war, and the four-to-one United Nations disarmament subcommittee of the 1950's. Now the Russians have asked for a five-five-five ratio, and one can guess that a compromise will be negotiated, eventually if not now.

So the parity principle has been faithfully reflected in Soviet policy for several years now since the time when it was discovered that, as the Chinese Communists were fond of putting it, "the wind is blowing from the east rather than from the west." But like so many trends, it took something special to dramatize it. The Congo supplied the requisite drama as well as the conclusive reason for the Soviets to demand the extension of the principle of parity to the office of the Secretary General. The Secretary General had since 1955 been virtually an independent diplomatic power in the Middle East. That process accelerated during and after the Suez crisis when the United States, for one, was delighted to believe that important elements of policy could be left to Mr. Hammarskjold. And perhaps the straw that broke the Marxist back was not the Congo but Laos in its earlier international incarnation, i.e., in 1959 when the Secretary General followed up the Security Council subcommittee by himself sending and keeping on the scene a United Nations *presence* in the form of successive high-ranking Secretariat officials.

By the interior logic of Soviet doctrine, as the Secretary General became more and more of a political force in world politics in recent years, it was inevitable that the institution his office represented would require revision to reflect the realities of world power. The matter then reached a head in the Congo, where the Russians found they could no longer tolerate the position of independent strength reached by Mr. Hammarskjold, enabling him for the first time actually to thwart an important Soviet Union policy objective. The death of Patrice Lumumba supplied the trigger for activating a policy which undoubtedly reached deeply into ideological depths.

There is, of course, nothing remotely new in Mr. Khrushchev's recent assertion to Walter Lippmann that, while there may be neutral countries, there are no neutral men, and that he would never entrust the security of the Soviet Union to any foreigner.[3] Maxim Litvinov used to say that only an angel could be neutral and there were no angels. That the security of Russia should be placed in the hands of someone else has always been unthinkable. The historical background thus places in a rather more complex light the assertion that the Russians want to destroy the United Nations. It also gives a more sophisticated meaning to Mr. Khrushchev's more recent statement that for the United Nations to be an effective medium for settling international disputes, "treatment with very good medicine" must be undergone so that it would not become a "weapon for imposing the will of one state over another."[4] Finally, it means that American diplomacy faces the task of a battle for control, which in many ways is harder and more complex than a defense of the United Nations against its outright destruction.

The Soviets have never pretended to achieve their objectives all at once. In the years when the votes were 55 to 5—a situation

[3] *New York Herald Tribune,* April 17, 1961.
[4] Speech at Yerevan, May 6, 1961; *New York Times,* May 7, 1961.

Americans would have enormous difficulty in adjusting to under reversed circumstances—Soviet representatives managed to rationalize their defeats into victories, or at the very least publicly pretended that it did not matter. In more recent years departing Soviet representatives have tended to be downright euphoric. If the campaign to convert the Secretariat does not succeed this year, next year will do, or the next. Thus speaks a state with a plan, and in the state of mind that Edmund Wilson once described as that of a man going upstairs on an escalator.

Implications of the New Veto

The parliamentary ability of the United States to block the Soviet's crude attempt to dump Mr. Hammarskjold and substitute a three-headed monster is not really in doubt. What is truly disturbing is the implication of this campaign for situations in desperate need of nonpartisanship. What is really discouraging is that the Soviet doctrine of partisanship should become so emphatic at a time when the world increasingly needs third parties in the form of neutrals who can interpose themselves between belligerents, and men who can be trusted by both sides. This development is going to make it increasingly difficult to sustain the recent development of patterns of third-party interventions in issues depending on Soviet assent or co-operation. Perhaps its most serious implication is in the field of arms control and disarmament, given the tripartite veto the Soviets are currently seeking to impose in place of neutral direction of inspection and verification machinery in a nuclear test ban treaty.

I myself have never worried very much about the question of

great power veto in the area of sanctions in connection with disarmament agreements. If there is an egregious violation, if the disarmament—or test ban—agreement is breached, other nations will act to protect their own interests, whether by rearming or seeking to negotiate anew or both. It would not matter much if there were a great power veto over sanctions: the action taken would correspond to the existing political and power realities.

But a veto on the internal operations of the inspection machinery is as crucially important as it is relatively unimportant regarding sanctions. For here the security of nations participating is to at least some degree dependent on the assurance that they will receive timely, reliable, and objective information that the parties are in fact complying. It is out of the question that an inspection and verification system could work if one of the sides were in a position to veto its detailed operations. This prospect, like the prospect of a crippled Secretariat operation, makes for pessimism about the Soviet version of coexistence.

But we are not required to accept either. We have the option of insisting upon the concept of a single, neutral administration—which may result in paralysing much of the operation if no compromise is reached—or we can explore the possibility of giving greater weight to the various power factions while retaining the central principle of neutrality.

It is possible, even likely, that compromise plans and arrangements will be suggested, possibly as a follow-up to Mr. Nehru's abortive suggestions in 1960. It is possible that some formula for a cabinet-type system, or for elected deputies (reviving an earlier Dumbarton Oaks proposal) or for magnified advisory committees, etc., will be adopted and prove tolerable. Essentially reciprocal inspection, with perhaps some neutral nation participation, may be the pattern for such limited arms control agreements as can be reached in the near future (which incidentally gives great urgency to the need for rapid technological development of robot sensing, monitoring, and reporting devices and systems). The nations themselves may have to revert to a more active role in the investigation and observation of disputes and situations, as under the League of Nations and indeed in the United Nations under the Lie administration.

But even with the greatest attempt to be reasonable and to acknowledge in symbolic ways the changing realities of the international power order, the underlying principle that is at stake cannot be compromised. Part of the ethical and intellectual tradition of the West is that men *can* be impartial and fair-minded, even as between nations. Such edifices of international jurisprudence as have been built attest to that conviction. We must, I believe, stand absolutely firm on our refusal to submit to Khrushchev's dictum that there are no neutral men. His assertion that this is true should not be accepted any more than the late Mr. Dulles' equally unhelpful dictum that neutralism was immoral. So long as parliamentary power still lies with us and not with the Russians on precisely this sort of issue, we should guard zealously our stewardship of this one precious advance out of the jungle in international relations and actively nurture it at every opportunity in places that do not require Soviet assent.

Summitry at the United Nations

There are many other facets of the diplomatic problem in the United Nations that one might discuss if there were time and space. A word might particularly be said about the suitability of the United Nations as a site for summit meetings. The performance in the early part of last fall was superficially a tribute to the drawing power of unilateral diplomacy. But the spectacle of ten heads of state, including one king, and thirteen prime ministers, fifty-seven foreign ministers, and some other fourteen cabinet ministers of other rank all present and competing for public attention holds obvious dangers both for the United Nations and for the kind of accommodations between nations which, when one really gets down to it, is the goal of diplomacy and the road to easement of international tension. I happen to believe that the United Nations can be useful for summit diplomacy if it is conducted seriously out of the public gaze, as in fact some of it *was* conducted in 1960 in New York. The Security Council under Article 28 can hold periodic meetings with high governmental figures present and can under its rules hold closed sessions. Such a procedure can be invaluable when bilateral channels break down; certainly it could be an important method of keeping decision makers in touch with one another. The danger of using the 99-member Assembly for this delicate task is obvious.

Concluding Comments

There is nothing easy about America's diplomatic task in the United Nations today. If we used to be, as Dean Rusk liked to put it, the fat boy in the canoe, we have slimmed down considerably. Power has become diffused and is likely to become more so. The metaphor can be varied. To the extent that political corpulence means satisfaction with the status quo, our ultimate objective, to steal a phrase from Alistair Buchan, should be fat Russians and fat Chinese. But the road is a long one, and so far they both wear a lean and hungry look. We can take some comfort from their disparate rate of maturity and from their growing internal tensions. One can take more than a little satisfaction from the Soviet doctrine enunciated by Mr. Khrushchev on January 6 of this year that seems to rule out military solutions in the form of what he called thermonuclear and limited wars.

But there is a large joker in the deck of peaceful coexistence, for the same doctrine enthusiastically endorses communist manipulation of "wars of national liberation." For the United Nations this can only spell a continuous budget of ambiguous, muddled, and otherwise sticky situations of civil war, indirect aggression, guerrilla warfare, subversion, and the like, all capable of escalating into larger conflicts, and the treatment of which will require the highest order of diplomatic skill whether bilaterally, regionally, or through the United Nations.

The United States had the best of both worlds for a while. It enjoyed the virtuous sense that world order was in process, however slowly, along with the comfortable conviction that it would be pretty much all our way except for a small handful of outlaws. Things are no longer so simple. Of course there are things we can do to make a minority position less likely for the United States, chiefly by pursuing policies of liberalism and sympathy toward the growing majority of states and by identifying ourselves more closely with their interests as they themselves interpret their interests. We can make the minority role less likely for ourselves by foregoing our traditional insistence upon victory in all matters, however peripheral; I am thinking of the inordinate amounts of diplomatic capital squandered in election fights, minor adjustments in rates of contribution to the budget, and meaningless rhetorical declarations in United Nations resolutions. We have conditioned ourselves to winning on every point, and such a situation, if it ever really existed, has now vanished. We can relax on the purely symbolic matters—which mean so much to some others—and focus our energies on the new operational potentialities of the organization where our security interests *are* deeply involved. We can give the new countries more rather than less responsibility to accelerate their maturing process. We can oppose the Soviets on their corrupting reforms and work gladly with them on matters of common interest.

But in spite of our best efforts, we cannot surely predict the future. Above all, we cannot be sure whether the presently ominous portents and trends in the United Nations scene represent a cycle—like so much else in history including the history of the United Nations—or a spiral, taking us to wholly new and unpredictable diplomatic, military, and institutional places. For what comfort it brings, things have actually been worse before—and the game is by no means over yet.

4

SHIFTING INSTITUTIONAL PATTERN OF THE UNITED NATIONS

by

ERNEST A. GROSS

A BRITISH political observer has said:

"The United Nations does not carry on power politics in the ordinary sense of the word—it is arrangement politics. This reflects something which is of considerable interest in the world today, namely the decline of power politics which goes with the decline of the Security Council."[1]

The comment was recently quoted and elaborated upon by Lester Pearson, as follows:

"At this time, when the forces of social and political action can be as explosive as an uncontrolled nuclear reaction, we have nothing more certain to guide our progress than the politics of arrangement between nations and blocks of nations . . . there is no other practical focus for our aspirations."[2]

Reference to the so-called "decline of power politics" is of

[1] Address of William Clark to Royal Institute of International Affairs, 19 January, 1960; *International Affairs* (July, 1960).

[2] Address at University of British Columbia, 2 February 1961.

particular interest, because many would say that, on the contrary, there has never been a time when power was more essential to national survival. Nevertheless, the nuclear stalemate necessitates re-definition of the traditional concept of "power," according to which primary weight is given to *military* power, that is to say, to the mere capacity to deliver force.

"Politics of arrangement," on the other hand, refers to the task of dealing with sources of disorder while working at the sub-structure of order. Mr. Pearson reminds us that this process requires "an understanding of the techniques necessary to effect political, social, economic and cultural change without recourse to force." Organization and application of such techniques materially affects power relationships among nations, in the context of our times.

The following analysis of the shifting institutional pattern of the United Nations proceeds from this point of departure.

The changed complexion of United Nations membership, reflecting revolution and aspiration, the political chemistry worked by the nuclear deadlock upon the means and ends of national power as well as upon regional arrangements, and discernible shift of political tides within the Communist bloc—all these developments, and many others, have resulted in changes in role of the principal organs of the United Nations, both internally and in relation to each other.

This discussion deals with some of these changes in the Security Council, the General Assembly, and the Secretariat.

The Security Council

The reference, quoted above, to the "decline of the Security Council," implies that the Council at some stage attained a height it could not hold. It is perhaps more accurate to say rather that, in the light of its hoped-for purposes, the Council has, from the beginning, been a glorious failure. The framers of the Charter in many ways showed realistic awareness that the plan could not succeed without an unprecedented degree of self-discipline, particularly on the part of the permanent members of the Security Council.

The reserved power of the veto was a safeguard against involvement. But it was also a challenge to responsibility. Proof that the unanimity rule is not in itself an evil is found in the Convention of the Organization for Economic Co-operation and Development, signed December 14, 1960. The like-minded members of the Organization insisted on the veto, not only with respect to decisions, but recommendations as well. The larger powers regard the veto as a defense against irresponsibility; the smaller as a safeguard against coercion.

The early evolution of the Security Council was one of the clear signals of the developing Cold War. Deadlock on implementation of Article 43 coincided with Soviet rejection of the British and French invitation to participate in a joint program for the economic recovery of Europe. Both events took place in 1947.

By reason of the failure to reach agreement on Article 43 forces, the Security Council never acquired legal competence to exercise responsibilities under Article 42, that is to say, to "take such action by air, sea, or land forces as may be necessary to maintain or restore international peace and security." This was one of the deliberate gaps in the Charter, designed to be bridged by Article 106.

Article 106 provides: "Pending the coming into force of such special agreements referred to in Article 43 as in the opinion of the Security Council enable it to begin the exercise of its responsibilities under Article 42, the parties to the Four-Nation Declaration, signed at Moscow, October 30, 1943, and France, shall, in accordance with the provisions of paragraph 5 of that Declaration, consult with one another and as occasion requires with other Members of the United Nations with a view to such *joint action on behalf of the Organization* as may be necessary for the purpose of maintaining international peace and security." (Italics added.)

Secretary of State Stettinius, in his Report to the President on the United Nations Charter, expressed the intention of the United States, clearly: "Only the power to take military enforcement action is withheld from the Security Council and that only temporarily. The 5 powers which will be permanent members of the Security Council are granted authority to fill the *temporary vacuum* to the extent necessary by taking action on behalf of the Organization."

No special agreements under Article 43 have come into force. The obstacles to their consummation are precisely the same as those which have prevented the "transitional security arrangements" envisaged in Article 106 from filling the security vacuum. The vacuum is not, of course, one of institutional or mechanical inadequacy, but of irresponsibility.

Frustration of the Council

The Security Council has been deformed from birth. It was an early casualty of the Soviet revolt against the Charter, more familiarly known as The Cold War.

It is scarcely remembered that in June, 1950, the Security Council lacked juridical authority to take military enforcement action in Korea. Hence, it limited itself to making recommendations, although in somewhat equivocal language. The Article 106 gap had not then been filled, and has not been filled since.

This fact, coupled with continued abuse of the veto, marks the major shift in the institutional pattern of the Security Council. These are symptoms of the anemic state of the international order and defy mechanistic solutions.

Nevertheless, the Security Council has an important, though reduced role to play. Its potential value lies in the fact that it is the forum of first recourse in the normal crisis, if one may use these words in conjunction. It was the Council which dealt initially with the Congo, and adopted the first three resolutions, which have been the basis of action ever since.[3] Mr. Hammarskjold has pointed out that constant talks and negotiations among members "have given the Council a continuing life and importance and enabled it to exert its influence during the intervals when it does not meet in public."[4]

Any doubt about the prestige value of Council membership is dispelled by the often bitter competition for too few seats. Increasing pressures for enlargement of the Council to meet the requirements of the new membership also evidences a general feeling of the importance of that Organ. No doubt such an increase, perhaps by adding three new members, would be a sensible thing. It seems unlikely that the Soviet government will accept a Charter amendment to that end until the Chinese representation issue is solved. Nevertheless, we should continue to press for such an enlargement. It should not be assumed that the Soviets will not relent. Their 1949 walk-out, on the ground the Council was illegally constituted without Red China, did

[3] Resolutions of 14 July, 22 July, and 9 August, 1960. (The Soviet Union concurred in all three.)

[4] Introduction to Annual Report of the Secretary-General, 14th Session; August 1959.

not preclude a walk-back six months later, on some unexplained, though no doubt dialectically sound, reasoning.

Like his predecessor, Mr. Hammarskjold has suggested the organization of regular meetings of the Council in executive session. However, Article 28, paragraph 2, remains one of the dead letters of the Charter and seems likely to remain interred. The possibility of Summit meetings around the Council table has a latent appeal, although arranging a confrontation of Khrushchev and Chiang Kai-Chek would be one of the more difficult exercises in the art of "arrangement politics."

In sum, the Security Council has, from the start, been an organ of maneuver rather than of power. The Uniting for Peace Resolution,[5] which was designed to enable the General Assembly to act more promptly and effectively in meeting threatening situations, merely signalled an obvious condition. The preponderance of power once envisaged for the Council has never been marshalled. At the same time, because of Soviet abuse of the veto, it was necessary to curb the Security Council's power to obstruct cooperative action.

The Council's power to initiate cooperative action will always remain vulnerable to abuse of the reserved right to veto. However, this merely proves that there is no realistic alternative to self-discipline.

Finally, it would seem prudent, from the standpoint of our national interest, to discourage resort to the Council on matters in which the Soviets can play the old game of keeping their intentions to themselves, inducing compromises of questionable principle, and then jumping in any direction they choose when the time comes to vote. For example, when the Soviet government suddenly turned the Kashmir question into a cold war

[5] Resolution 377 (V); 3 November, 1950.

issue, the Security Council became an unsuitable forum for consideration of the matter.

The New Role of the General Assembly

Analysis of the shifting role of the General Assembly usually begins with consideration of the Uniting for Peace resolution[6] and of the impact of the new membership. Although both of these are decisively important factors, I venture to say there is an even more suitable starting point: that is, the function of public debate in multilateral diplomacy.

In the conclusion of his "Parliamentary Diplomacy,"[7] Judge Philip C. Jessup quotes Wilfred Jenks' comment that "one of the crucial tests of the wisdom of an international constitutional practice is whether it is calculated to promote and facilitate agreement or to provoke occasions for unnecessary disagreements . . . (and) a sterile majority vote achieved by parliamentary maneuver but ineffective in practice."

When Senator Vandenberg hailed the Assembly as "the town meeting of the world," he was no doubt thinking in the American tradition of the local taxpayers assembling in small towns, to call the tune. This was a classic exemplification of community in action.

Comparison of the Jenks and Vandenberg comments reveals differing approaches which are instructive in considering the institutional role of debate in the General Assembly. The former, a craftsman of multilateral diplomacy, emphasizes sound techniques for negotiation. The latter, a seasoned politician,

[6] *Ibid.*
[7] Hague Academy of International Law. Recueil des Cours. 1956, p. 316.

stresses the importance of processes which strengthen a sense of community. As is true of human institutions generally, there is need for a constant search for balance between the short and long range objectives and for processes which further one without defeating the other.

Untimely and unrestrained debate has indeed "provoked occasions for unnecessary disagreements," as Mr. Jenks says. However, much depends upon who is passing judgment on whether, and when, disagreements are "unnecessary." Denial of debate has often stoked the fires of a volcano, which later erupted with a force earlier outlets might have moderated.

Ten years ago the French Government took it as an unwise and unfriendly act when the United States favored discussion of Morocco and Tunisia in the United Nations.

Five years later, in June, 1955, the Premier of France pledged to the French National Assembly that his Government would "never agree to renounce, negotiate about, or admit to question, the French position in Morocco. . . ." The following year, Moroccan independence became a fact of international life.

In 1954, the British Government opposed United Nations "interference" in the Cyprus question, insisting it was solely an internal British affair, even though it involved a bitter quarrel between Greece and Turkey. After resolution of the dispute, Prime Minister Macmillan avowed it had always been an "international" problem.

The history of these matters is surely relevant in appraising the present contention of Portugal that international concern in the future of Angola is an unwarranted intrusion upon Portuguese privacy. Indeed, the Government of Portugal has seen fit to attribute the tribal terror in Angola, and harsh reprisals therefor, largely to provocation engendered by United States support for the Resolution on Angola in the 15th Session of the General Assembly.

While he was Chief of the Permanent Mission of the United Kingdom to the United Nations, Sir Pierson Dixon complained of undue United Nations interference in colonial issues. He argued that "the mere discussion of such topics in the great forum of the United Nations can have a profoundly disturbing and even damaging effect in the territories themselves." Nevertheless, Sir Pierson neglected to suggest practical standards by which to judge when, in particular situations, discussion would cease to be disturbing or damaging, or, indeed, whether even more disturbance and damage might flow from imposed silence.

More recently, President de Gaulle has reviled "tumultuous and scandalous meetings" of the General Assembly. He called for "organizing an objective debate" in the United Nations. President de Gaulle, likewise, failed to suggest standards of objectivity, or to say who is to take charge of organizing the debate.

Countervailing Views of the Assembly

On the other hand, the States of Asia and Africa—from the 1955 Bandung Conference to the present—have manifested their will to employ the forum of the United Nations for the purpose of airing matters high on their own agenda of concerns. From their perspective, denial of discussion is more often a tactic of power than a device of moderation. Ingredients which make debate "disturbing and even damaging" in the eyes of a colonial administration may, in themselves, affect power relationships. An example, cited elsewhere in these pages, is the effect of annual General Assembly debates of conferring a kind of recognition or "legitimacy" upon the Algerian FLN.

The United States is thus confronted with a recurrent dilemma which must be faced with candor. At times we have attempted to evade dilemmas by the device of abstaining from controversial resolutions. Unfortunately, we cannot thus easily escape the consequence of our power and influence.

An inevitable consequence of refusal to identify the Assembly with struggles for self-determination is to weaken its capacity to take constructive action in the troubled after-math of such struggles.

Post-independence needs of emergent states confront the General Assembly with what might be called the second-generation problem of colonialism. By what standard of political realism could the United Nations take a "hands-off" attitude when a people are struggling for freedom, yet aspire to win their confidence and cooperation when their political aims have been won?[8]

If we lived in a different kind of world, such a question might be regarded as irrelevant, or even unrealistic. But the communist prowler rarely foregoes an opportunity to move in on chaos, when the international community moves out.

Perhaps the decisive shift of the institutional pattern of the United Nations consists in the fact that its principal organ has become a popular revolutionary assembly, in the eighteenth-century sense of the term. De Gaulle's strictures against "tumultuous meetings" comes strangely from the leader of a nation whose parliamentary history is marked by the tumult of its meetings and, indeed, is a fountainhead of popular assemblies everywhere.

Impatience with disorganized and interminable debate comes

[8] The role of the United Nations in helping to build new states is the theme of Joseph E. Johnson's paper, to which the above comments form a mere footnote.

readily to the delegates who have become weary watchers of the night. But the dynamics of current history fully justify Mr. Pearson's reference to the need for "understanding the techniques necessary to effect political, social, economic and cultural change without recourse to force." The key words are the last four.

When we feel harassed by the tumultuous meetings of this popular assembly, we should remember that the practical alternative is not "organizing an objective debate," as called for by the President of the Fifth Republic. The alternative is reversion to a feudal, pre-revolutionary period, when debate was not "organized" but outlawed.

It may seem like belaboring the obvious to pursue this matter further, but I venture to say that our future attitude toward the United Nations, and our posture in it, may center largely upon our analysis of this institutional development. Of course, if Sir Pierson Dixon, President de Gaulle, and Dr. Salazar are right, the alternatives are correctly posed as a choice between supporting debate or supporting our friends. It is, however, just as easy—and much closer to the truth—to state the matter just the other way round. If the approach of our friends is wrong, it is they who face a choice of either accepting debate or undermining our common interest.

Of course, in politics there is no absolute standard of right and wrong and, as the saying goes, there are times when one must "rise above principle." But, inasmuch as we are discussing a shift of institutional pattern from, if one may say, the self-disciplined "town meeting" to the restless popular assembly, it seems essential to have a perspective around which friends can really—or at least, can agree on what they are refusing to rally around.

One final thought on this point: the shift in pattern of the Assembly is undoubtedly of most serious consequence to the Soviet Union. Their original conception was, of course, that the Security Council would deal with matters of political consequence and the General Assembly confine itself to generality and propaganda. Soviet opposition to the Little Assembly and Uniting for Peace Resolutions was expressed in constitutional terms, and viewed as dangerous encroachments upon the Security Council.

The pattern of Soviet behavior at the 15th Assembly to some extent reflected frustration with the pattern of the institutional development. There is a wide-spread feeling among Delegations, that Soviet tactics at the United Nations have not been successfully geared to their strategy, and that the smaller states, far from being fooled, have rallied on vital occasions to Hammarskjold and to principle.

Permanent Delegations

A corollary of this evolution—or preferably, this growth—of the Assembly, is the establishment of permanent United Nations delegations. This is, in itself an evolved institutional pattern of unpredicted importance.

It has made possible a diplomatic contribution which, Hammarskjold has said, "may well come to be regarded as the most important 'common law' development which has taken place so far within the constitutional framework of the Charter."[9]

This development is a prime reason for adequate staff and facilities for the United States Mission to the United Nations, and justifies the high priority now being given to rebuilding

[9] Introduction to the Annual Report of the Secretary General; 14th Session; 20 August, 1959; p. 2.

our Mission to the United Nations, under Ambassador Stevenson's leadership.

There is a dual significance to the establishment of permanent delegations with senior representation. One is that, in a formal sense, public sessions have assumed less importance in the hammering out of agreements. There is an old saying that debates in the Assembly sometimes change opinions, but rarely change votes. As Mr. Hammarskjold has noted, the Assembly has increasingly become a forum for "public confrontation of views which have developed in negotiations under other forms, and for the registration of a resulting consensus, or, when this has not been achieved, of a difference of opinion with the relative support apparent from the votes."[10]

The United States should take note of this diplomatic evolution, which places a high premium on seeking a balance between conference diplomacy and private negotiation, since the two are on most occasions mutually supporting. It has been a traditional defect of our diplomacy that we have underestimated the need for carrying on "U.N. diplomacy" in the world's capitals—that is, to do our homework for the General Assemblies on a twelve-month per year basis, and at all places in which we

Response of the Secretariat

In the principal capitals, there might well be attached to our diplomatic mission a United Nations specialist, with primary responsibility to advise concerning items on the agenda of the General Assembly or other organs, and to assure that full advantage is taken of bilateral diplomacy to support our multilateral efforts.

[10] *Ibid.*

Structural Problems

From the standpoint of its own organization and processes, the General Assembly has in the main preferred *ad hoc,* or temporary agencies, to fixed and permanent ones. The latter are few in number and innocuously non-political, such as UNICEF.[11] When agencies designed for service of limited duration prolong their existence it usually means that the problems with which they are connected have defied solution. Examples range from the Relief and Works Agency for Arab Refugees, created in 1950, to the United Nations Emergency Force (UNEF), set up on short order to meet an emergency, which is now five years old.

The expansion of United Nations membership and the enlargement of the agenda justify close study of methods to improve its institutional processes. Many suggestions have been offered to rationalize voting techniques, curtail and avoid duplication of debate, endow chairmen with greater authority, limit agendas through screening committees, and so on. Continuing study of these matters is important, frustrating though it may be. The Assembly rostrum offers too good an opportunity to be lightly foregone in the name of efficiency.

Nevertheless, the more attention is paid to the devices of discipline, the more aware participants become of infringements of the code. Self-discipline is a by-product of self-study. If for no other reason, the Question of Improvement of Procedure should be a perennial item on the Assembly's agenda. Each year a Special Committee of highly respected individuals should be designated to study and report to the following Assembly.

[11] The Advisory Committee on Administrative and Budgetary Questions and the Committee on Contributions are provided for in the Rules of Procedure of the General Assembly.

Such a continuing emphasis would not only focus attention upon the requirement of self-discipline, but could also provide yardsticks of conduct which might—over the years—tend to become a common law for the Assembly.

Moreover, it would help to put into proper focus such essentially formulistic devices as weighted voting, or standing inter-sessional committees.

As to the former, it may fairly be said that the very emphasis upon the *weighting* of voting, in itself tends to give too much significance to the *process* of voting. Inasmuch as the General Assembly is limited to making recommendations, there would seem to be merit in stressing the substance of agreement, rather than the arithmetic of the ballot. Here again, a common law can be shaped by putting first things first. In any event, the difficulties involved in working out an equitable formula which would meet with the approval of the great powers—to say nothing of the smaller states—make clear that little progress may be expected in the direction of weighted voting.

Attempts to establish standing inter-sessional machinery, to facilitate the business of the General Assembly, have proved abortive. The Interim Committee, or "Little Assembly," met 46 times in the three years after its creation (1947-1950). It has not been heard from since. Because of Soviet opposition, on grounds of asserted illegality, the Little Assembly simply has not fitted the requirements of "arrangement politics."

The Peace Observation Commission, hailed by the late Secretary of State Dulles in 1950 as the "eyes and ears of the U.N.," has been employed only once, when a team was sent to the Balkans in 1951 at Yugoslav request. It then disappeared from view so completely that no thought was given to its use in the Hungarian crisis—even during the week the Imre Nagy government was appealing for help. UNEF was organized for Suez overnight and sent to Gaza—but in Budapest the United Nations remained eyeless.

Such abortive efforts to set up standing machinery show the chasm between mere formula and actual practice. They may serve as object lessons to exponents of world government or federalism, proving how difficult it is in politics to work from preconceived patterns or ideal forms. They recall Pope's couplet: "For forms of government let fools contest; That which is best administered is best."

On the contrary, in areas of the most critical concern, the General Assembly has resorted less to planned devices than to the tactics of ambiguity. On one occasion, the Secretary-General, with an unprecedented lapse from elegance of expression, reminded a group of delegations that because "a matter is controversial is not a sufficient reason to pass the buck to the Secretary-General, or for the Secretary-General to pass the buck back to the General Assembly."

Largely in response to such appeals, a new institutional device has emerged in the form of consultative committees, or similar organs, which can share some degree of responsibility with the Secretary-General. This was done, for example, in the first Assembly resolution on UNEF during the Suez crisis.

The United Nations Advisory Committee on the Congo has proved to be one of the most important institutional devices yet created, since it has successfully served as a bridge between a hopelessly ambiguous mission and an infinitely complex problem. Faced with a governmental task, comprising military, political, economic and social elements, the Secretary-General constantly has been exposed to contradictory accusations of doing too much or too little and, in either case, doing it wrong.

Not long ago, Mr. Hammarskjold informally described this as playing lottery. He wondered whether, when action was required, and merely ambiguous instructions were given to the Secretary-General to support necessary action, it might not be wise "to let the major organs themselves take the responsibility for inaction."

The reference to "responsibility for inaction" is a lightning flash, illuminating a major shift in the institutional requirements of the United Nations. *Inaction* has become the source of grave danger. Statement of this proposition provides a suitable point of departure for a discussion of the role of the Secretary-General.

The Secretary-General

The Secretary-General has long regarded the United Nations as performing dual functions: those of an organ of negotiation and those of executive organ.[12] From the standpoint of the Secretariat, the latter has meant increasing use of military, police, diplomatic, and administrative functions. The former has been manifested in mediation activities, which have been described as the modern counterpart of third-country good-offices of an earlier period.

The sum of these two functions approximates executive responsibilities typical of most national systems. In some respects, the duties are similar, although in rudimentary form, to those carried out by administrative agencies in the United States, with quasi-judicial or rule-making power.

[12] For example, his speech at Copenhagen on 1 May, 1959 (U.N. Press Release SG/812).

As outstanding examples, the administration of Palestine refugee assistance and arrangements for the Congo operation, itself patterned generally after UNWRA, require for their accomplishment an energetic Executive. And it has been the American tradition from the beginning that the prime requisite for energy in the executive is unity.

Alexander Hamilton might have been discussing the Soviet proposal for a three-headed Secretariat, when he wrote in the *Federalist* (70): "Decision, activity, secrecy and despatch will generally characterize the proceedings of one man in a much more eminent degree than the proceedings of any greater number. The unity may be destroyed . . . by vesting the power in two or more magistrates of equal dignity and authority. . . ." Hamilton concluded by saying that experience "teaches us not to be enamoured of plurality in the Executive."

It would be hard to think of any system less enamoured of plurality than that of the Soviets. And motives may fairly be suspect when a person, or a group, reserves one standard for its own business, yet applies a quite different standard to the business of others.

It is, of course, the Soviet objective to weaken the United Nations Executive by the device of plurality in the form of a triumvirate. Although unhappy from the beginning by the concentration of authority in one person not under their control, the chemistry of dialectical materialism did not make the institution itself unacceptable until the frustration of Soviet objectives in the Congo. Khrushchev no doubt concluded that Hammarskjold was a "murderer" long before Lumumba's death, because Khrushchev had come to regard the Secretariat itself as a sort of Murder, Incorporated.

It is often said, and quite accurately, that the Soviet assault on the Secretariat is a blow aimed at the institution itself and confronts the United Nations with its gravest crisis. Perhaps the matter can be stated with greater precision, without losing too much of the drama.

The Soviet Challenge

The issue which really confronts the membership is this: will it remain possible to continue the evolution of the office of the Secretary-General so as to enable the Organization to provide for necessary action, which otherwise might not be open to it? In other words, will the members permit themselves to be coerced by the Soviets into surrendering their most practicable safeguard against "responsibility for inaction"?

Destruction of this means of necessary action would have many consequences, predictable in the light of the very reasons why the office has evolved. The evolution has, of course, been in response to a need, not the result of a reach for power.

Smaller nations tend to be swayed by the thought that the Secretary-General should be a "bridge" between East and West and that a bridge ceases to be of much use if it is severed in the middle. This view stresses the use of the United Nations as an organ of negotiation, and almost completely ignores its function as an executive organ. It is based on the fallacy that the Soviet Government would be more amenable to compromise and conciliation, if only it had "confidence" in the Secretary-General or his office.

It may be difficult to persuade them of the fallacy. But they would, I believe, readily understand a summary of some predictable consequences of stunting or deforming the office.

The record of recent years shows at least three major categories in which the growth of executive power has taken place.

In each of these, the interests of small powers are heavily involved.

The first, already referred to, is the creation and successful operation of administrative agencies for economic assistance, for relief, policing or other government type services. The principal beneficiaries of such functions, usually costly ones, are the peoples and governments of the smaller countries.

Secondly, the "good offices" function, through multifarious forms of the "U.N. presence," has essentially served the purpose of assisting smaller governments in threatening situations. In this field, the Secretary-General has most often acted upon his own initiative—the prime characteristic of energy in the Executive. This, in turn, has obviated the need for formal decisions by organs of the United Nations—decisions which, if prerequisite to action, would frequently involve awkward debate, damaging delay or mischievous intervention.

Thirdly, as pointed out above, the Secretary-General has assumed responsibilities on the basis of ill-defined and often deliberately ambiguous terms of reference. All members have been beneficiaries of his skill and devotion to duty in such tasks. We have only to think of his mission to Peiping, undertaken in 1954 on the basis of a resolution which, simultaneously, condemned the Red Chinese government and asked the Secretary-General to negotiate with them. The pattern was repeated in his South Africa mission, pursuant to the Security Council resolution of April 1, 1960 on the Sharpeville case.

Response of the Secretariat

In surveying such a range of responsibilities, one is struck by the essential loneliness of the office. Mr. Hammarskjold himself has contrasted his position in this respect with that of the

Executive of a national government. In the latter case, he has said, the Executive "has the assistance of a group of close collaborators who represent the same basic approach and to whom he therefore can delegate a considerable part of his responsibilities."[13] However, in the case of a universal organization in a divided world, the political and diplomatic tasks entrusted to the Secretary-General, particularly those based upon vague terms of reference, require him to discharge his duties on a quite personal basis.

Reorganization of the Secretariat seems inevitable, and is probably healthy—provided always that the integrity and energy of the office is preserved. In the words of Prime Minister Nehru, addressed to the General Assembly: "If the executive itself is split up and pulls in different directions, it will not be able to function adequately or with speed. . . . At the same time, the executive has to keep in view all the time the impact of various forces in the world, for we must realize that unfortunately we live in a world where there are many pulls in different directions."[14]

It would be difficult to improve on this formulation of the dilemma. There is not likely to be an easy consensus on the form of organizational change, although the growing awareness on the part of the smaller powers that their interests call for an effective United Nations makes drastic change unlikely. Given a basic confidence in the integrity and motives of the incumbent Secretary-General—which he has earned many times over—it is likely that in the end the solution will be left to him, as has been true so often in the case of other dilemmas.

[13] Address in Chicago; 29 April 1960 (Press Release SG/910).

[14] Statement by the Prime Minister of India in the 15th General Assembly of the United Nations, 3 October 1960.

On balance, it would seem desirable to seek flexible and variable processes for dealing with the "many pulls in different directions," of which Prime Minister Nehru spoke. No single reorganization formula is likely to be adequate. It would either be destructive—like the Soviet triumvirate proposal, or ineffectual—like the suggestion of vesting specific duties in particular offices, or corrosive—like ordaining a limited number of Deputies, each to represent a "different direction."

Functional Internationalism

The objective of strengthening the executive might be furthered by placing greater emphasis on what the late Anne O'Hare McCormick used to call "functional internationalism." In complex political issues, the advantages of the Advisory Committee technique have proven themselves, as in the cases of the Suez and the Congo.

Similarly, in the scientific and technical fields, select committees have shown their value, within the areas of their assignment. These have included such diverse bodies as the Scientific Advisory Committee, the Scientific Committee on the Effects of Atomic Radiation, the Ad Hoc Committee on Peaceful Uses of Outer Space, and others. All of these have given valuable assistance in the performance of technical and executive functions.

The role of the specialized agencies has been widely debated, and the desirability of coordinating their activities often pointed out. Nevertheless, there is much to be said for building up their Secretariat and Executive functions. This might well prove to be a safeguard against possible chaos in the event the Secretariat of the United Nations were weakened—particularly after the expiration of the term of the incumbent Secretary-

General. Their strength and resources could always be pooled and coordinated, given the will on the part of the principal contributors to do so.

In sum, it would be unwise to concentrate on any single approach or formula. The alternatives are not either to unify or to fragment the Secretariat. The answers must be found in identifying each task and devising the means most suitable for dealing with it.

Concluding Comments

This paper has sought to deal with certain basic elements in the shifting institutional pattern of the United Nations. Probably the strongest pressure encouraging a positive strengthening of the functions of the United Nations is the need of the underdeveloped countries for assistance in advancing their economic, social and political progress. On the other hand, there are powerful countervailing forces of conflicting national interests, especially the animosity of the Soviet bloc toward any effort that would thwart their own special objectives. It is this clash of contrary purposes that will largely shape the future institutional evolution of the organization.

The three councils—the Security Council, the Economic and Social Council, and the Trusteeship Council—continue to provide smaller forums of selective composition to give intensive consideration to certain problem areas and to exercise leadership in their respective jurisdictions. They suffer, however, from the absence of any acceptable system of representing the full membership, which problem has been accentuated by the sudden influx of new states, and from the severe tensions that divide some of the countries. The fact that the General Assembly is fully representative makes its deliberations more acceptable to many of the Members, but, at the same time, makes its deliberations extraordinarily awkward, time-consuming, indecisive, and tempestuous.

Tumult in this fumbling parliament reminds us of the traditionally primitive character of all assemblages struggling toward the creation of law. Rousseau noted that the task of legislation involves two incompatibles: "an enterprise too difficult for human powers, and, for its execution, an authority that has no power."

The impatience of the founding father of the French Fifth Republic is not more eloquently expressed than that of a founder of our own Republic. James Madison registered his distress in the *Federalist* (37):

"The history of almost all the great councils and consultations held among mankind for reconciling their discordant opinions, assuaging their mutual jealousies, and adjusting their respective interests, is a history of factions, contentions, and disappointments, and may be classed among the most dark and degraded pictures which display the infirmities and depravities of the human character."

The statement might well be hung over the gateway to the United Nations, along with a well-pounded shoe.

An invaluable corrective for some of the deficiencies of the General Assembly and the three councils is the Secretary-General and his staff. Where the collective bodies are splintered, dilatory, and indecisive, the Secretariat is relatively united, efficient, and decisive. It cannot, of course, go far beyond the limits set by the political bodies, but, within those boundaries, it has demonstrated its capacity to help provide more effective policy and administrative leadership than has been forthcoming from any other quarter of the United Nations.

Given this situation, it behooves the United States to strengthen the capacity of the United Nations to pursue the objectives of the Charter which are the same basic purposes that guide United States policy.

5

THE CONTAINMENT AND RESOLUTION OF DISPUTES

by

INIS L. CLAUDE, JR.

IN A MULTISTATE WORLD, disharmonious relationships among states—not among all states, all the time, but among some states, some of the time—are to be expected. International unpleasantness is a matter of degree; it ranges, and may progress (or, from the standpoint of a peace-lover, regress), from a set of conditions likely to breed trouble, to reasonably well-defined disputes, to situations of overt conflict. Conditions, disputes, and conflicts: these terms designate critical points in the development of inter-state troubles. To put it differently, we might identify pre-dispute, dispute, and post-dispute stages.

The United Nations was directed by its Charter to undertake trouble-inhibiting activity at each of these stages. Broadly speaking, the so-called functional activities of the United Nations and the specialized agencies are designed to deal with conditions; pacific settlement relates to disputes; and collective security pertains to the conflict, or post-dispute, stage.

The efforts of the United Nations to forestall the development of disputes by ameliorating the general condition of the global body politic fall outside my terms of reference. This paper deals with the actual and possible role of the United Nations in the latter two stages. In practice, of course, these three stages are not neatly distinguishable, and a given bit of unpleasantness may not follow the indicated pattern of metamorphosis. Nevertheless, I hope that my scheme may prove valuable as an analytical device.

The Resolution of Disputes

The Charter represents an attempt to create an organization capable of giving effective assistance to states in the peaceful settlement of disputes. In this connection, I suspect that one of the major crosses which managers of American foreign policy have had to bear since 1945 has been the insistent advice to avoid the sin of "by-passing" the United Nations. One has heard a good deal of the naive faith that the United States can simply take its burdens to the United Nations and leave them there, a viewpoint which is sometimes attached to the dogma that nothing worthwhile in international relations ought to be done unless it can be done through the United Nations. I have scant respect for this brand of internationalist piety, and I note that the Charter itself invites states to by-pass the United Nations so far as possible in the quest for peaceful settlement of disputes. I presume that American officials are more likely to be annoyed than swayed by this kind of preachment, and can be counted on to persist in their willful pragmatism, judging in each case whether solution of a dispute is more likely to be attained in the

United Nations or elsewhere. One must hope that those who know the United Nations best—those most familiar with the outer and inner limits of its possibilities—will have a fair share in the shaping of those judgments. I suspect that American policy is at least as likely to be influenced by uninformed disdain for the United Nations as by undisciplined enthusiasm for it, and I suggest that we need in government a considerable body of men who are able to moderate between these two equally unhelpful attitudes and to bring to bear on decisions concerning diplomatic tactics a sophisticated understanding of the potentialities and limits of the United Nations forum.

One must also hope that decisions to use or not to use the United Nations in particular cases may be made in the awareness that the development of the organization's capacity for future usefulness depends heavily upon the use which is made of it from time to time. The anti-by-passers have a point in their suggestion or implication that American national interest is involved in the long-term evolution of the United Nations as well as in the short-term settlement of disputes and solution of problems; concern for immediate results must be balanced by concern for gradual improvement of the institutional structure of world order. I hasten to add that this consideration does not necessarily militate against by-passing the United Nations in a given case. Whether the development of the organization's effectiveness will be furthered or hampered by its being entrusted with a particular problem is a question of judgment. All that can reasonably be asked is that both the objective of achieving satisfactory solutions of specific problems and that of promoting the healthy development of the United Nations be taken into account, and that the officials best qualified to judge the existing potentialities and developmental problems of the United Nations be given a prominent role in the consideration of alternatives.

The Nature of International Disputes

In principle, the peaceful settlement of disputes is a matter requiring agreement among the parties. Today, this may mean agreement among interested and indirectly or covertly involved parties—allies, supporters, supervisors of satellites, and the like—as well as and perhaps even more than agreement among the states ostensibly engaged in controversy. In principle, again, the occasion for singling out a "guilty" party and attempting to discipline it by sanctions arises only at the conflict, or post-dispute, stage. Peaceful settlement involves voluntary agreement of the parties; collective security involves compulsion of a party. In practice, an objective observer may have difficulty in distinguishing between the dispute and conflict stages of an affair, and thus in determining whether attempts to promote agreement or to impose discipline are in order; it should occasion no surprise that politically motivated statesmen, subjectively engaged as they are likely to be, have even greater difficulty in reaching consensus on the character of a troubled situation and the appropriate functional response of the United Nations.

Assume that a dispute exists, and that an attempt at peaceful settlement is in order. Clearly, the function of the United Nations is not to settle the dispute, but to encourage and assist the parties to reach an agreed solution. At this point, we need to know what resources are required for the production of that result, and which of those resources the United Nations may be able to supply. The attempt to answer these questions brings us immediately to the recognition that disputes vary in their characteristics; the stable of international controversy houses horses of many different colors. There are disputes which are genuinely isolated concerns of small states. There are disputes in which great powers are indirectly involved on one or both sides. There are disputes between a great power and a small state, or between great powers, or between groups of small states; the possible combinations are many. There are acute and chronic disputes, disputes which carry an imminent threat of violence, and disputes between states which are most unlikely to fight each other. There are disputes within alliance or regional families and between such families. There are disputes within jealously guarded great-power spheres of influence and in the open country of world politics. There are disputes which are raised in order to be settled and those which are not so raised. This list could obviously be extended at great length.

Resources for Peaceful Settlement

It should be clear that different kinds of disputes require different resources for their settlement, and that the United Nations has a varying capacity to make helpful contributions. So far as one can generalize in the face of the variety which I have incompletely described, I would say that the requirements for peaceful settlement include these major items: incentive, communication facilities, diplomatic skill, and mediation.

In no case can the United Nations serve as the exclusive supplier of these essential ingredients. In many cases, however, it may be able to make useful and even indispensable contributions. On the record, it has done so in a number of instances, and it may have done so in some cases where its contribution was too subtle to be generally recognized.

Let us consider the element of incentive to reach an agreed settlement. Mutual perception of relative power positions by the parties is relevant here. Who would win a war, if it came to that? To what degree would the other party be able to enlist allies to supplement his military strength? There is no reason to suppose that diplomats have abandoned the traditional practice of looking over each other's shoulders to discover what power is there to back up policy. Nor can it be asserted that the United Nations makes very much difference in this respect. In the setting of the United Nations, states may develop and exercise their capacity to attract allies and supporters, and they can hope that fellow members of the organization will be induced by their loyalty to the principles of the Charter to fight beside them in case of aggression. But no state can sensibly operate as if it were assured that the combined power of all or most of the members of the United Nations would be brought to its support in case of unjust attack; by and large, power relationships are determined outside of, and without reference to, the world organization.

Relative power, however, is not the sole factor in incentive to settle, or to engage in genuine negotiation of a dispute. The danger of *losing* a war is rapidly being matched in cautionary significance by the danger of *having* a war; the self-interested urge to avoid pulling the world down around one's national ears is becoming more and more compelling. Again, this danger—which one hopes will operate powerfully as an incentive to seek peaceful solutions—is a function of national weaponry, not of international organization. However, United Nations debates may serve to strengthen its deterrent effect. The organization provides a forum within which many voices are raised to remind disputants that both self-interest and moral responsibility demand that they not set off World War III, and to warn that even little wars between little states might lead to that catastrophe. The United Nations is a place where it is insistently proclaimed that war is illegal, immoral, and irrational, where statesmen are loudly warned and, what is no less important, quietly cautioned not to be rash, or irresponsible, or stupid. Unhappily, statesmen are not all equally sensitive to pressures of this sort, or equally reluctant to gamble with the fate of humanity. Nevertheless, it is important that we have, in the United Nations, an instrument for the mobilization of collective concern. The first task of the United Nations is to help states to want, and to recognize the vital necessity of achieving, settlement of disputes without violence.

Avoidance of war is a negative achievement; peaceful settlement of disputes requires positive action, which can best be described as the process of negotiation. This process requires effective communication among persons qualified to represent the interests and viewpoints of their governments. The channels of communication provided by the United Nations are, of course, merely supplementary to the network which exists on the outside; most governments which want to engage in diplomatic talks have a variety of choices. However, the value of these particular channels deserves thoughtful consideration. They are most important to new states which have not developed and perhaps cannot afford to develop a universal diplomatic network. They may have special value in disputes which involve numerous parties and therefore require multilateral negotiations. They may be especially needed in cases where tensions prevent the maintenance of normal diplomatic relations on a bilateral basis, or where only informal contacts on neutral ground seem politically feasible. New York has become a beehive of diplomatic activity, some of which could not take place at all, and much of which could not be conducted as well, in other settings.

Diplomatic skill cannot, of course, be manufactured by an international organization. Its development may, however, be nurtured by the sort of experience which national spokesmen gain through service in the United Nations, and its utilization may be facilitated by the collegial relationships which they develop within the United Nations context. The United Nations is a peculiar, and perhaps a peculiarly important, educational institution for diplomats; we should not discount the possibility that its old school tie may become important in international relations. The task of maximizing the development of, and optimizing our utilization of, the United Nations as a diplomatic setting is a challenging one.

Finally, there is the ingredient of mediation; parties to disputes may need the assistance of relatively disinterested third parties. The ultimate function of the United Nations in this realm is to facilitate agreement among statesmen who have, for whatever reasons and in response to whatever pressures, developed a genuine urge for peaceful settlement. It can provide facilities, formal or informal, institutionalized or improvised, for promoting accommodation and enhancing the prospects for stability of settlements once reached. The United Nations is, *par excellence,* a collection of third parties, a setting within which states not involved in disputes may exercise whatever conciliatory influence they may possess or be capable of generating, and render all possible assistance to disputants who experience difficulty in finding the mutually acceptable solutions which their sense of prudence may impel them to seek. Moreover, the organization has created, or has been in process of evolving, what might be called artificial third parties—instrumentalities other than states, staffed by personnel formally committed to represent the general international interest—with important peace-promoting potentialities. It has available for instant use, or can manufacture on urgent demand, a variety of devices that may be serviceable for facilitating negotiated settlements or for implementing agreed arrangements. Indeed, I would suggest that one of the great values of the United Nations lies in the fact that it provides the world with a well equipped and well staffed workshop, capable of designing and producing such mechanisms as may be required for dealing with international problems in the political as well as other fields.

Role of the UN in Resolution of Disputes

An objective evaluation of the actual functioning of the United Nations must deal with three categories: utility; futility; and disutility. Efforts to extract national or international political value from the institutions and processes of the United Nations may often be futile; in dealing with disputes, the organization can be used to encourage states to seek, and to help them to find, solutions, but it cannot dictate the seeking or guarantee the finding. It is equally clear that the United Nations can be, and has been on occasion, misused so as to exacerbate rather than to conciliate differences, to hinder rather than to promote adjustment. The problem of avoiding this effect involves not simply the question of *how* the organization should be used, but also the question of *whether* it should be used at all. The prospects for solution of some disputes may be diminished by the mere fact of their being placed in the multilateral hopper. More typically, however, the crucial question relates to the manner in which the resources of the United Nations are brought to bear upon a dispute.

There is doubtless room for improvement in the techniques of peaceful settlement employed under United Nations auspices; one might, for instance, argue for the revival of the *rapporteur* device which the League of Nations developed. One might insist that the critical problem is to persuade states to make greater use of such existing mechanisms as the International Court or the Peace Observation Commission. However, it seems to me that the most urgent requirement for enhancing the effectiveness of the United Nations as a promoter of peaceful settlement is one which pertains to the general conception of the pacifying process, rather than to the development or utilization of particular techniques. All too often, the United Nations is treated as a political battlefield where victories are to be won, rather than as a conference table where accommodations are to be reached. It is used as an instrument of denunciation, not conciliation; the aim is a massing of votes, not a meeting of minds, the passing of a resolution, not the working out of a solution. A parliamentary triumph in the United Nations is no substitute for diplomatic success, and may in fact impede diplomatic success.

It is perhaps too much to hope that parties to disputes will refrain from seeking largely illusory victories in the United Nations in favor of allowing the organization to function in a manner more conducive to pacification. Indeed, the world is so full of political contests that it would be naive to expect the

United Nations not to resound with disputation; the sound of polemics is reassuring evidence that the organization has not lost touch with the real political world. Moreover, there are occasions when collective castigation of an international offender, ineffective as it may be, seems inescapably appropriate.

However, a successful drive by one party to secure the international condemnation of its opponent's position and endorsement of its own is in general the worst possible prelude to efforts at peaceful settlement. If, as I have suggested, this is nevertheless the ambition which most parties to disputes are likely to exhibit, the solution would seem to lie in the possibility that relatively disinterested parties might dominate the proceedings of the United Nations when disputes are brought before it.

The manner in which the United Nations deals with a dispute ought to be controlled by statesmen—national and international—who aim at the promotion of accommodation, not by contestants who aim at exploitation of propaganda advantage. Third parties should be less frequently members of an audience to which first and second parties address their arguments and appeals for support, and more frequently leaders of a movement to have the United Nations proceed in such a way as to prevent the exacerbation, and promote the settlement, of disputes. We have heard too much, and seen too little, of the role of small and uncommitted states as conciliators. I am aware of the fact that disinterested parties have sometimes played such a role in United Nations proceedings, but when I survey the long list of cases in which the organization seems not to have exploited to the full its settlement-promoting potential, I am inclined to believe that it might have been more effective if its facilities for enabling third parties to engage in mediation had been given greater prominence over its facilities for enabling first and second parties to engage in mutual recrimination.

Such a shift of emphasis as I am suggesting will require a combination of initiative and assertiveness by disinterested parties, and acquiescence on the part of interested ones. I doubt that it can be achieved by the formulation of new rules and procedures. What is needed is the development of a general awareness that the United Nations can facilitate the resolution of disputes only if it is treated less as an arena where the antagonists conduct the battle and more as a chamber where the peacemakers seek to find the basis for an acceptable truce. Blessed are the peacemakers—if they get a chance, or seize a chance, or make a chance, to assert their pacifying influence.

I should stress the point that I attach limited significance to the peaceful settlement of disputes under United Nations auspices as a device for promoting order in today's troubled world. I do not believe that all disputes can be eliminated if only the world organization is properly and skillfully used. I do not suggest that all apparent conflicts of interest can be shown to be artificial if only the voice of the general international interest is permitted to be heard. I do not insist that either justice or order requires that all differences between states be split down the middle. Concretely, I recognize that there are conflicts of interest within the framework of the Cold War (and elsewhere) which probably cannot be resolved in the foreseeable future, and that there are conflicts of purpose and principle between the Soviet and Western groupings which should not be resolved by expediential compromise.

The modest claim which I make for the United Nations in regard to international disputes is simply this: it can assist states in finding settlement of disputes if they seek settlement, and it can be used to dramatize the common interest in seeking such diminution of tensions as may be essential to the avoidance of general war. If it promotes the idealization of indiscriminate compromise, it may render us—and everybody—a disservice. If it facilitates the recognition and exploitation of genuine opportunities for reducing the danger of war, it will render us—and everybody—a great service.

The Containment of Disputes

Let me turn now to the containment of disputes, or, more accurately, of difficulties which are at or near the conflict stage. When disputants have arrived at this fateful brink, the issue is no longer whether they can be helped to get together but whether they can be kept apart. The task is to impede resort to violence rather than to facilitate negotiated agreement.

In the standard theory of international organization, the diagnosis of conflict is supposed to involve the discovery of an aggressor, and the obvious prescription is a dose of collective security. In these terms, the ideal function of an international organization is to deter or suppress aggressive violence by mobilizing collective sanctions of whatever type may be required. Thus, the degeneration of disputes into conflicts is to be prevented or reversed.

Collective Security

It is clear, though it has often been forgotten or overlooked, that the founders of the United Nations, taking a hard look at the world that was about to emerge from World War II, abandoned the notion of attempting to apply the collective security prescription in any general sense to that world. In adopting the unanimity rule for non-procedural issues in the Security Council, they announced that the organization should not be put in the position of attempting to implement collective security against, or against the will of, any of the major powers. At most, as Chapter VII of the Charter indicates, they contemplated collective action in conflicts which might find the Big Five united in the desire to permit and take action—in cases, that is, of relatively minor importance in world politics. Even this limited version of a collective security system has not been erected. Despite the continued ideological hold of collective security upon most theorists of international organization, this doctrine is largely irrelevant to the United Nations as it has developed and as it seems likely to develop. We may find it difficult to talk about the United Nations without expressing the assumption that it ought to be, even if it is not, an agency for the collective suppression of aggression wherever it might occur, but in truth there seems to be little genuine and active commitment to the realization of that ideal. As for the United States, I take it that we do not propose to leave the question as to whether or not we will react militarily to expansionist moves by the major Communist powers to the decision or the indecision of the Security Council or the General Assembly, and that we are not attracted by the idea of having armed forces from those powers sent into trouble zones as agents of the United Nations. I should be the last to take up a stand of doctrinaire adherence to the principle of collective security in opposition to this position. We are not alone; for one reason or another, virtually every member of the United Nations finds the notion of the organization's functioning as a collective security agency an ideal suitable only for liturgical use.[1]

In suggesting that collective security has been brushed aside by members of the United Nations, I do not deny that the *doctrine* has left an imprint upon the organization and upon the thinking of contemporary statesmen. This imprint is evident in the general acknowledgment that international aggression (however poorly defined that concept may be, both in the abstract and in the circumstances of particular cases) is reprehensible, and that any aggression is everybody's business, given the interdependence of destiny which links all states and makes the maintenance of international order a vital interest of every state. Moreover, the moral pressure of the consensus which is registered in the United Nations in opposition to the arbitrary use of force may have, in particular cases, a considerable deterrent effect. It must be recognized, nevertheless, that states rely upon security arrangements developed, unilaterally and multilaterally, outside the United Nations, for prevention or repulsion of aggressive challenges to their independence. However significant the ideological residue of the doctrine of collective security may be, the crucial fact is that, apart from the Korean experience, the United Nations shows few signs of becoming a means for translating that doctrine into an operational system, capable of mobilizing collective force to shield any victim of aggression against the impact of any attacker. Such a system might be desirable, but it does not exist and I see no prospect of its coming into existence.

[1] I have developed this analysis more fully in "The United Nations and the Use of Force," *International Conciliation,* No. 532, March 1961.

"Preventive Diplomacy"

What then, if anything, can the United Nations do about disputes or situations that threaten to break open the Pandora's box of international conflict? Over time, a new function for the organization has been evolved, one which is well described by the phrase, containment of disputes. It has been most explicitly performed or undertaken in the Suez and Congo crises, by the military forces organized and utilized by the United Nations in those delicate situations. It has been most perceptively articulated by the Secretary-General, under the rubric of "preventive diplomacy."

This new role for the United Nations involves the use of military units supplied by states other than the great powers and so far as possible unattached to the major Cold War blocs, under the executive leadership of the Secretary-General, in the effort to stabilize situations which might otherwise tend irresistibly to attract the competitive intrusions of the East and the West. The objective is to insulate the affected areas, to neutralize them, to prevent their becoming zones of chaos and conflict which might invite the spreading and worsening of the Cold War.

Mr. Hammarskjold has postulated that:

> As a universal organization neutral in the big-power struggles over ideology and influence in the world, subordinated to the common will of the member governments and free from any aspirations of its own to power and influence over any group or nation, the United Nations can render service which can be received without suspicion and which can be absorbed without influencing the free choice of the peoples.

He notes that "it is extremely difficult for the United Nations to exercise an influence on problems which are clearly and definitely within the orbit of present-day conflicts between power blocs," and therefore assumes that the primary usefulness of the United Nations lies in the possibility that it can aid in "keeping newly arising conflicts outside the sphere of bloc differences." He defines preventive diplomacy in terms of putting the world organization into a given situation outside of, or on the margin of, the Cold War, "so that it will not provoke action from any of the major parties, the initiative for which might be taken for preventive purposes but might in turn lead to counteraction from the other side." Such collective intervention into unstable situations which might otherwise attract the competitive intervention of East and West is regarded by the Secretary-General as a means by which the organization may exercise "a most important, though indirect, influence on the conflicts between the power blocs by preventing the widening of the geographical and political area covered by these conflicts and by providing for solutions whenever the interests of all parties in a localization of conflict can be mobilized in favor of its efforts." The political basis for this United Nations activity is to be found in "the fact that both blocs have an interest in avoiding such an extension of the area of conflict because of the threatening consequences, were the localization of the conflict to fail."[2]

Two points should be noted: this function of preventing the addition of new areas to the zone of Cold War competition can be performed on behalf of the United Nations only by the relatively small and uncommitted member states; it can be successfully performed by them only if the major Cold War contest-

[2] All quotations are drawn from the *Introduction to the Annual Report of the Secretary-General on the Work of the Organization, 16 June 1959—15 June 1960,* General Assembly, Official Records: Fifteenth Session, Supplement No. 1 A(A/4390/Add. 1).

ants have a sufficient awareness of their stake in the mitigation, or the non-exacerbation, of that fundamental struggle to welcome or at least to acquiesce in its being done. It cannot be done *against* the major powers; it cannot be done *by* them; it can only be done *for* them and by their leave.

The Soviet Challenge

In the Congo case, the outcome of the United Nations venture in stabilization and neutralization remains in doubt. In general, the United States has seemed to understand and to support this effort; we have acknowledged and appreciated the value of keeping the Cold War out of the Congo. While the difficulties of the Congo operation cannot be laid at any single doorstep, many of them must be attributed to the Soviet Union. Of fundamental importance is the fact that the Soviets, after seeming initially to acquiesce in the project, subsequently developed a hostile attitude which has been expressed in attacks upon the Secretary-General, upon the basic concept of the Secretary-Generalship, and directly upon the operation itself, as well as in their refusal to contribute financial support.

The Soviet campaign has been variously described as an effort to destroy the United Nations, to weaken it—specifically, to undermine its capacity to conduct future operations similar to the one in the Congo—or to dominate the organization. At the least, it can be agreed that the Soviet Union has insisted upon making the Congo an area of Cold War competition, and has cast doubt upon the possibility of the organization's being able to implement the concept of preventive diplomacy in future situations. Our reaction has been to deplore the Soviet assault, to despair of the future of the United Nations if that assault should be permitted to succeed, and to resolve upon firm resistance. We must stand by Hammarskjold; we must save the executive capability of the Secretary-Generalship; we must solve the problem of financing ventures like that in the Congo, which the Soviets refuse to support financially or otherwise; we must not let the United Nations be deprived of the opportunity to develop this new and useful role.

It might be suggested that there are four major alternatives for the United Nations when political crises arise in areas outside the generally acknowledged spheres of interest of the two major powers—that is, in the "no man's land" of the Cold War. The organization may (A) take pro-Western action; (B) take impartial, neutralizing action; (C) take no action at all; or (D) take pro-Soviet action. In general, our order of preference runs like this: A-B-C-D. The Soviet order of preference, I believe, runs in reverse: D-C-B-A. It is not surprising that alternatives A and D appear at the opposite extremes in these two schemes; this is an inescapable fact of life. What is more significant, I think, is that alternatives B and C are reversed in the two patterns of priority. Typically, we prefer impartial action, neutralizing action of the sort attempted in the Congo, to inaction by the United Nations; the Soviet Union appears to prefer inaction—or paralysis, as we would describe it—to such action. Herein lies a critical problem.

Note that this generalization is restricted in application to cases arising outside the *de facto* orbits of the two blocs. In 1956, the United States supported the injection of the United Nations Emergency Force into the Middle East, rather than a United Nations policy of inaction which might have permitted the development of competitive East-West involvement in that area. At the same time, we acquiesced in the organization's restricting itself to hortatory action in the Hungarian case, presumably because we believed that the Soviet Union would not tolerate an attempt by the United Nations to neutralize (for Cold War purposes) a sector of the Soviet orbit. Subsequently, the United States and Britain intervened in Lebanon and Jordan, but pulled back in favor of stabilization measures developed under United Nations auspices, thus indicating an urge to avoid the danger of inciting the Soviet Union to intensive rivalry in that area. In April 1961, the United States sponsored and supported an abortive intervention in Cuba; in this instance, the United States clearly preferred inaction on the part of the United Nations, and would have been greatly embarrassed by a move for United Nations intervention of the UNEF or Congo variety. Cuba, of course, lies within the American orbit, not in the "no man's land" of the Cold War; American preference for inactivity by the world organization in this case does not violate my generalization. It should further be noted that the United States viewed its Cuban venture as a *counter*-intervention, an effort to combat what it regarded as an unacceptable intrusion of Communist influence, traceable ultimately to the Soviet Union, in our zone. American behavior in regard to Cuba does not reflect a preference for having Cuba left open as a locus for the free interplay of Cold War competition, but a demand that the boundaries of our bloc be respected. I suggest that all the cases cited are compatible with the proposition that, when critical instabilities arise in the area *between* the blocs, the United States tends to believe that it is better for the United Nations to take action designed to forestall the development of new foci of Cold War struggle, while the Soviet Union tends not to favor such action.

Why the difference? The United States, I would speculate, prefers B to C because it fears that C may either permit the world situation to degenerate so that major war will become likely, or tend in effect to become D—that is, inaction may work to Soviet advantage. Perhaps the United States also hopes that B will really turn out to be A—that United Nations interventions may serve Western interests in a more specific sense than simply keeping Cold War tensions under control.

Conversely, it may be that Soviet preference for C over B reflects a less cautious attitude than ours concerning the threat of World War III, a hope that C may turn out to be D, and a fear that B may have the effect of A. Soviet leaders may welcome the chance to wage the Cold War in the Congo and analogous situations, feeling confident that they can win it; they may regard United Nations action designed to inhibit the extension of the struggle as depriving them of an opportunity for victory in the Cold War. Looking at the Congo case, they may also suspect that the United Nations operation tends to favor—and perhaps that it is *intended* to favor—Western interests. If this latter proposition is plausible to a Westerner—and I suggest that it is—it may well be convincing to a Soviet official.

My point is that Soviet policy regarding the Congo operation probably reflects one or both of these convictions: that impartial international action is undesirable because it frustrates a Soviet triumph in the Cold War; that international action of the sort undertaken in the Congo is in any case not genuinely neutral, but pro-Western in import. Perhaps they do not believe in the desirability, and cannot believe in the possibility, of impartial United Nations action in such situations.

The American Response

This analysis leads me to reflect upon the appropriateness of our response to the Soviet attack upon the United Nations, an attack directed particularly against the organization's operational capability in cases of the Congo type. While, as I have suggested, the United States has displayed an urge to have the United Nations inhibit the development of new focal points of Cold War competition, this interest has always been secondary to our general commitment to the extraction of the fullest possible political value from the organization as a buttress to the Western position in the global struggle. To revert to my alphabetical formula, our preference for B over C has been overshadowed by our preference for A over B. Our occasional insistence that it is both desirable and possible for the United Nations to function as an impartial agent, serving the real interests of both sides by filling a vacuum neutrally and thereby reducing the tendency of Cold War blocs to move into it competitively, has been confused and made less credible by our more general tendency to regard the organization as an instrument to be used by the West in the struggle against the East. The ambiguity cuts deep into our own thinking; we should like the organization to be able to alternate between serving Western interests and presiding with what everyone must regard as majestic impartiality over the interests of the contending blocs.

It must be stressed that the bulk of our policy with regard to the United Nations has been directed toward enhancing its usability as a Western instrument. We have a long history of insisting that the United Nations ought to be able to act, even, if necessary, in the face of Soviet opposition. This is to say that we lost little time after San Francisco in repudiating the implication of the veto rule, which is that the organization should *not* be capable of taking major political action opposed by a major power as contrary to its interests. In a nutshell, the history of the United Nations is a record of American attempts to destroy or reduce the meaningfulness of the Soviet veto power, and of efforts by the Soviet Union to maintain or increase the efficacy of its veto. Having created an organization with a built-in, and deliberately designed, impediment to its operating in situations of great-power disunity, we have persistently undertaken to make it operable in just such situations. Our evaluation of the United Nations has rested heavily upon its potentiality for being transformed into an agency capable of acting with Western support, regardless of possible Soviet objections. Our recent anxieties about the organization stem largely from the recognition that the era of Western dominance in its political processes is passing, or has passed.

Both our devotion to the task of enabling the United Nations to override Soviet opposition to programs and activities projected by the West, and our past successes in that undertaking have diminished the credibility of our claim that the organization should be viewed by all as an agency capable of rendering invaluable neutral service in such cases as the Congo. The Soviet Union entered the United Nations with serious misgivings about the minority status which it saw in prospect for itself, and its extreme sensitivity to direct and indirect attacks upon the veto power is indicative of the value which it places upon this formal reassurance against the organization's being turned against Soviet interests. In practice, we have so valued our opportunity to use the United Nations as an instrument of Western policy that we have tended to rub the Soviet Union's nose in the fact of its minority status. Rather than help the Soviet leaders overcome their long-standing doubts concerning the impartial quality of the United Nations, we have tended to strengthen their suspicion that it tends to function in support of Western interests, disguised as the general international interest. We have come face to face with the difficulty of having it both ways. We cannot value the United Nations, in general terms, as a pro-Western agency, and expect the Soviet Union to value it, at our occasional convenience, as an impartial agency of the international community. If the Soviet Union cannot believe that the United Nations is a neutral factor in the Congo situation, this disbelief may be the result of an ingrained attitudinal tendency reinforced by awareness of our commitment to using the organization for our purposes, and of our record of success in that respect. I do not mean to suggest that there is anything immoral or even abnormal in our disposition to use the United Nations so far as possible to promote American and Western interests; I do mean to suggest that our devotion to this general objective may defeat our hope of enabling the organization to gain acceptance as an agency transcending bloc partisanship in specific instances such as the Congo crisis.

Evaluation of the American Response

My conclusion is that we should discard our preoccupation with the problem of enabling the United Nations to act against Soviet opposition, in favor of a preoccupation with the problem of convincing the Soviet Union that it is both possible and desirable for the organization to serve the interests of both the major blocs, and of the world at large, by functioning as an agency for mediating between disputants and for confining the scope and moderating the intensity of the Cold War. As I see it, the usefulness of the United Nations as an instrument for taking action which we support and the Soviets oppose is small—and is rapidly becoming smaller. It is natural that the Soviets seek to incapacitate the organization for that role, and probable that they can achieve substantial success in that undertaking. This is to say that, in a fundamental sense, the philosophy of the veto which was espoused by the framers of the Charter was, and still is, realistic; if we continue to base our general United Nations policy upon a repudiation of that philosophy, we shall, I fear, be battering our heads against the stone wall of reality. Moreover, the harder we try to use the United Nations to oppose the Soviet Union's conception of its interests, the greater risk we will run of damaging its capacity for containing the Cold War. The tragedy which I see looming ahead for the United Nations is not that it may prove increasingly unable to act in the face of Soviet hostility, but that it may become less and less capable of recommending itself to both sides in the global struggle as an agency for serving such common interests as they may be induced to recognize in the settlement of disputes, reduction of tensions, and restriction of their areas of conflict.

In short, I think that our crucial task is to convince the Soviets, if we can, that impartial action by the United Nations to help keep the Cold War under control is both urgently necessary and genuinely possible. I am not, be it noted, denying the reality or minimizing the depth of the conflicts of interest and purpose which divide the Soviet world and ours. I am not suggesting that those conflicts can or should be neatly compromised or that competing interests can be buried under an avalanche of internationalism. I am not talking about "ending the

Cold War," desirable as that may be. My point is that we have a stake in persuading Soviet leaders that they have a stake in preventing the Cold War from getting so desperately out of hand that it might precipitate World War III, and in convincing them that the United Nations can function impartially in forestalling such aggravation of the Cold War.

I am not sanguine about our prospects for convincing the Soviets in these matters. Their hope for victory in the Cold War seems to outweigh their fear that the expansion and intensification of that struggle might lead to a mutually destructive thermonuclear conflict. They have, as I have suggested, a built-in tendency to doubt the validity of the United Nations' claim to neutrality in the Cold War, and our record of viewing and using the organization so far as possible as a Western instrument reduces our persuasiveness. It may even be argued, with some plausibility, that we have opted for an impartial United Nations only after losing our capacity to control it.

Nevertheless, the effort must be made. Judgments may differ as to the most effective means, or the most appropriate tactics, for convincing the Soviets that they have a vital interest in the containment of the Cold War which can best be served by permitting the United Nations to maintain and develop its capability for operations like that in the Congo. It may be that we should relinquish some of the symbolic manifestations of Western proprietorship of the United Nations, and concede in some measure to their demand for greater assurance that the organization will not act against their will. Contrariwise, it may be that we should adopt a policy of firm resistance to Soviet attacks and demands upon the United Nations, undertaking to defeat any and all proposals for modification of its operational capability in the hope that we can then confront the Soviet Union with the resolute insistence that it should, in its own interest, acquiesce in the organization's exercise of that capability. Still another possibility is that we should rely upon the relatively small and uncommitted states, which bear the burden of active responsibility for carrying out the organization's role in preventive diplomacy, to bring pressure upon the Soviets for acceptance of this role, and to give assurance of the disinterested character of the performance. I do not purport to be capable of deciding among these alternatives. My concern is that we should attain clarity in our own recognition that our basic political task in the United Nations is to realize the possibility of an organization which serves each side best by serving the common interest in containing the Cold War, and in our recognition that the task must be defined in terms of securing Soviet acceptance of this concept.

I have no disposition to regard the United Nations simply, or even primarily, as a setting for international cooperation; it is also, given the nature of world politics, an arena for international competition. We have a great deal of competing to do with the Soviet Union, and some of it will doubtless be done within the framework of the United Nations. Clearly, political battles will continue to be fought there, and we should continue to try to win them. It may on occasion be necessary to make the effort, and possible to succeed in the effort, to have the United Nations carry out operations and programs for which Soviet support cannot be enlisted. My position, then, is not an absolutist one, but one which suggests a revision of general attitude and emphasis.

I am profoundly disturbed by the threat to the development of the United Nations' political usefulness which has been posed by the Soviet Union in its attack upon the operational capability of the organization. In responding to this challenge, we must avoid the wholly natural but basically unsound urge simply to "defeat" the Soviet Union by contriving somehow to enable the organization to function without reference to Soviet consent or dissent. This is not a matter of surrendering to Soviet demands; it is a matter of surrendering to the facts of life. For it is a fact, I believe, that the importance of the things which can be done in or by the United Nations against Soviet opposition is minor compared with the importance of the activities which can be carried out only if, and to the extent that, the Soviet Union is induced to recognize them as conducive to a result compatible with its basic interests. In these terms, we should concentrate less on equipping the organization to override Soviet opposition than on enabling it to gain Soviet acquiescence in, or support for, its playing an essentially neutralist role—one which contributes not to the winning of the Cold War by one side or the other, but to the limitation of the scope and intensity of that struggle. In a world of conflicting interests, this is a common interest of vital importance.

6

THE CAPACITIES OF THE UNITED NATIONS

by

HARLAN CLEVELAND

THE RELEVANCE OF WHAT appears elsewhere in this volume is a splendid encouragement to those of us within government. We have a real need for advice on strategy from the intellectual community. The other chapters prove that this community is neither moribund nor enmeshed in the problems of the 1940's; that it is clearly grappling with the issues of the moment, and to some extent with the issues of next year and the years to come in the sizzling sixties. It is particularly encouraging to a person who has not taken a course in international law for two decades to find that the definition of international law has been extended effectively and well.

There seems to be far less concern today with those wonderful cases where A and B get married and have a baby on the boat, but you really do not know about the nationality of C because the boat was aground in someone's territorial waters. Rather, we now find international law centering on the day-today practice and the changing operations of international organizations. When it is said that the principal alternative to war-making does not lie in mediation, conciliation and so on, but in law-making, we understand that to mean not just the kind of law that gets to the International Court of Justice, but more often what we call administrative law, or the law and practice of evolving institutions. In this context, it is possible to discuss meaningfully the changing institution that is the United Nations and the contributors to this volume have done so at a number of relevant points.

The United Nations has also been spared in this volume from the hyperbole of its friends. Nowhere in these chapters is it argued that the United Nations is guarantor of peace, patron of liberty and sponsor of plenitude. A stranger who greeted Samuel Johnson with "Mr. Smith, I believe," was told, "If you believe that, you will believe anything." Yet what are we to believe? If Dr. Johnson is not Mr. Smith, who in fact is he? We have some clews.

The United Nations is not a guarantor of peace yet it has acquired an impressive capacity to act on behalf of peace and security. While far from being the patron of liberty, it has shown a capacity to befriend the oppressed—especially on the question of colonialism. The United Nations has also displayed a capacity to create those institutions that must precede plenitude in the developing nations. *Act, Befriend,* and *Create;* these are, at least, a beginning—an ABC of world order. We might remember Victor Hugo's Marius Pontmarcy who in *Les Miserables* fought on the barricades with "The Friends of the ABC." Those ABC were, in French, the homonymous *abaissés.* The "downtrodden" still need friends on the barricades and the United Nations has certainly proved to be one.

The Ethics of Mutual Involvement

These capacities of the United Nations owe their existence to the fact that the ethics of mutual involvement are such that multilateral action is often acceptable and even welcome in many cases where bilateral involvement would be impossible.

We are used to the practice, if not yet to the theory, of mutual international involvement. We know that Americans are deeply concerned with the affairs of dozens of nations, through technical assistance programs, military arrangements, business enterprises, missionary work, and voluntary agencies. We know that our cultural exports are matched by cultural imports—most North American party-goers think nothing of dancing for at least half the evening to the samba, the cha cha, and other imported rhythms which give some of us a kind of culture shock right on our own home town dance floors.

We know that our vigorous efforts to export merchandise are matched by foreign competition in our own market, competition which is sometimes so painful that it erupts in our politics as arguments about pottery, optical goods, garlic, small cars, watch movements, bicycles, or clothes pins.

We know that our interest in other countries' internal problems like land reform or budget administration is matched by the concern of foreign politicians with what we consider our "internal affairs"; leaders in every continent now feel at liberty to think out loud, within earshot of the international press, about desegregation in southern United States schools. When it comes to people crossing borders, the exodus of Americans has almost been matched by a flood of Europeans, Asians, Africans and Latin Americans into American schools, colleges, universities and industrial establishments. At the level of information the $100,000,000 a year which the United States Information Agency has been spending abroad is paralleled by vigorous efforts, financed from overseas, to participate in the processes by which we Americans make up our minds, especially on foreign policy issues. They range from the careful and effective work of organizations like the British Information Service to the well publicized histrionics of Mr. Khrushchev on a balcony at 68th Street and Park Avenue in New York City.

We can understand from our own experience that some forms of intervention are beyond the pale. Americans generally were persuaded that it was hardly appropriate for a foreign power to maintain on our soil a political party whose allegiance was abroad. If a foreign country were to establish here a lobby for the unilateral abolition of nuclear weapons, or an alien group were to set up a technical assistance project to help the American organizations that are fighting for desegregation of public education in the South, even Americans who agreed with the objective would feel that the methods somehow went too far.

When the shoe is on the other foot, and Americans are working in other people's backyards, we also feel that an ethical line has to be drawn. It is all right to help set up an agricultural extension service, but the visiting American expert would probably be thrown out of the country if he started making campaign speeches for or against political candidates in a local election.

Some forms of intervention, then, are beyond the pale. But who decides the boundaries of the pale, and on what criteria? We need to develop an ethics of mutual involvement. And I suggest that one will be found, in fits and starts, by trial and error, in the growing body of practice by international organizations.

The Capacity to Act

The most striking thing about the United Nations and the most hopeful thing for the future of an organized world community, is that the ethical restrictions are realistic and as a consequence the United Nations has developed a large and rapidly growing *capacity to act.* It has demonstrated that an international organization can in fact mobilize funds and people for economic development, that it can put together a military force and a group of civilian administrators to bring a modicum of order and security where there might otherwise be civil war and communal rioting and chaos.

Each time the Organization takes on a new and bigger task, the skeptics wonder if it can survive the test. If the World Bank had tackled the Indus project ten years ago, it might have failed. If the United Nations had tackled the Congo or even the Gaza Strip ten years ago, it is questionable whether it would have developed the executive leadership to carry it off.

But now, after smaller political and military try-outs in several parts of the Middle East, the community of nations has come face-to-face in the Congo with the question of whether it can develop and make internationalism operative and effective. It is a big operation, involving 20,000 troops, and several hundred civilian administrators. It is scheduled to cost at least $120,000,000 this year.

It might have been more logical and more orderly to proceed from the Gaza Strip to the Congo in smaller steps developing more gradually the United Nation's military and administrative capability for field operations, instead of having to put together so large a field organization in one giant executive stride. It is a tribute to the nations who have served on the Security Council that they not only made it possible to start in the Congo, but they continued and strengthened the mandate when the going got rough.

It is a tribute above all to the imagination and pertinacity of Dag Hammarskjold that he did not shrink from this opportunity to show that an international organization can act as well as talk. Even the Soviets found a backhanded way to express their admiration: in their impugning attack on the Office of the Secretary General, they said they would refuse to "recognize" him—unconsciously using about a Secretariat official the language usually reserved in diplomacy for relations among sovereign states.

If you take the three major country crises, Cuba, Laos, and the Congo, it appears that the only one where we seem to be getting somewhere in finding an answer to the "war of liberation," as the Communists call their indirect aggression, is in the Congo. This may, and probably is, correlated with the fact that in the Congo our power and the power of others is being exercised in an international framework, where the ethics of mutual involvement permit overt rather than clandestine action. And this, too, leads us back to the problem of how we work in a world where mutual involvement is important and inevitable. For the newly-emerging areas the question is not whether external power is going to be applied in their internal affairs, but whose external power is going to be applied and to what degree.

It can be played one of two ways: the Spanish Civil War way, or by developing the capability of a third party to intervene and make the business of indirect aggression so notorious that it falls of its own weight. In the Congo, the communists have been falling over United Nations furniture that they did not realize was scattered around the room. They thought they knew where the furniture was. But then the United Nations upset many of their assumptions and brought enough strength in so that it was hard to move anywhere without tripping over it. This is a response to indirect aggression by the world community, more or less as a whole, that naturally is very bothersome to the communists and to which they have taken rather vigorous exception.

The Congo operation has helped to develop the law, the tradition, the practice, that mutual involvement in internal affairs is of increasing importance in less-developed areas. What has to be done is to develop rational and agreed forms of involvement or partnership or participation or whatever you may wish to call it. From this point of view international organizations, and notably the United Nations, represent the synthesis; they represent the way you get out of what the Marxists would call our contradiction on this subject. This to me is the significance of the Congo operation. It may never happen the same way again, but it has helped establish the principle of a monopoly channel of involvement. This monopoly excludes the Soviets and also excludes us; but we can live with this reciprocity because we want to be excluded and they do not.

And we can live with an operation pursuant to the purposes of the United Nations Charter. The words, the concepts and the principles that we are heir to are natural to mankind and it is therefore natural that when broad, internationally-agreed concepts are developed, they tend to be congenial to us and to our traditions. Indeed, it ought to be taken as a tribute rather than otherwise that when the Russians want to describe slavery they use the words of freedom; they have to use words of freedom, otherwise they could not make a sale, but in the process they take serious risks.

If the Congo operation can be maintained long enough, and strong enough, to set the Congo on a new path of relatively peaceful politics, there is more executive work ahead for the United Nations. There will be other vacuums to fill with pacifying troops and administrative know-how and economic aid. And there might be other kinds of operations: eventually, for example, an international control system for the hundreds or even thousands of satellites hurtling through the heavens.

Our Soviet friends are alarmed by the demonstration that an international agency can develop the capacity to act, and act on a substantial scale under emergency conditions. They prefer the sort of competitive bilateral intervention in which each victory takes the form of a "compromise" by splitting a weak country in half and establishing another miserable satellite on earth. And in the longer run, they are alarmed by the possibility that the growing operational capability of the United Nations to carry out a Charter which is full of dangerous thoughts about freedom of choice for all men, may simply bury the Communist version of history—without even a major war being necessary.

This is why the Soviets have zeroed in on the Secretary General. They know, from their own administrative experience as well as from the experience of bureaucracies everywhere, that executive power can only be effectively organized if some one person is ultimately in charge. They know that to put a committee in charge of a complex operation is a device for making sure that the operation will sicken fast with timidity and indecision, those universal symptoms of administrative failure.

But there is today in being a United Nations operation. There will have to be more and better ones in the future. That is why we also need to help the United Nations get itself organized, in the field of technical assistance and investment financing, so as to bring its many instruments to bear more effectively in support of each country's economic development program. That is why we have to press for cooperative operations in many fields of scientific and technical exploration.

That is why, finally, it is possible to distinguish between phony disarmament proposals and real ones. The real ones will contain plans for an international organization with the capacity to act—to inspect, to control, to publish, perhaps even to restrict to international use some of the more dangerous of mankind's toys. The phony proposals will be those which envisage a sweeping legislative act by the parliament of man,—like the Soviet proposal to "ban the bomb"—but cripple or reject the executive follow-through.

A criterion for every action we take that affects the United Nations system of organization might be: does it enhance, or does it tend to destroy, the Organization's capacity to take executive action?

The Capacity to Befriend

The United States cannot, of course, subscribe to every United Nations decision that may contribute to the three capacities described herein. To a certain extent we have to relax and accept the inevitability of debates in the United Nations that deal with the internal affairs of western industrialized countries as well as those of underdeveloped states.

The key thing to watch and worry about in the underdeveloped areas is their internal affairs and any analysis of the United Nations that neglects these is a little old-fashioned. It is too easy for us to keep our eye on the kinds of diplomatic issues that come up in the United Nations and not see them as an emotional reaction possibly stemming from frustration in the under-committed areas with respect to the problems of government. We are past the point in most areas of the world where raising his hand and shouting "Independence" is the mark of a leader. Now that we have come to the age of administration in these areas, things are getting much more difficult. It is in this frame that the phrase, "the United Nations is a school for political responsibility," becomes a very important piece of wisdom. The United Nations does teach that politics is real and earnest but even more important is what the United Nations can do, what we all can do, to assist in developing responsible government within the states themselves. This again raises for us the problem and the principle of mutual involvement in the affairs of the nations. From this perspective at least the United Nations is not primarily a mediation and conciliation service, or even a forum for arrangement politics. In most situations, both the emerging countries and the conscience of the world community want change, not a rearrangement of the *status quo*.

The purpose of the United Nations is much better expressed in the Charter which has to do with the freedom of the individual and the opportunity of people to grow up and fulfill their own aspirations.

Our trouble is the traditional codes of ethics and morality do not apply very well to the new kinds of problems we now confront. The traditional forms of intervention across cultural or national boundaries have been ethically contained not so much by consideration for the intervenee as by respect for the imported ethics of the intervenor. Until quite recently, says John Llamenatz of Oxford University, "the Europeans, in their behavior toward other people, have been restrained almost entirely by their own principles (whether shared with others or peculiar to themselves) and very little by respect for what was foreign to them." The traditional ethics of mutual involvement has been inner-directed, not other-directed.

Nowadays the pendulum is swinging, if anything, too far the other way. In revulsion against the notion that the outsider should make up his own ethical restraints as he goes along, the idea has become popular that the outsider should be bound, not by the criteria he finds in his own culture and tradition, but by the ethics of the culture which he is serving as technician or administrator. The intervenor can presumably tell whether he is overstepping those mysterious bounds by making sure that whatever he does is done at the request of the intervenee. Clearly interference is not interference if the state involved invites or accepts it.

But this criterion, too, presents some difficulties of administration. Who, for example, are "they"? The government? The people? Which people? And even if this question is resolved by assuming that every government effectively represents all of the people over whom it has jurisdiction, a fundamental problem remains. The fact is that most of the less-developed areas do not find in their own traditions and cultures all the elements of a code of ethics for handling the participation in their affairs of willing and ambitious advisers from the outside. The very reason for wanting advisers is to achieve more "development" or "modernization"—but "development" is not just a matter of techniques and equipment, it requires also a revised set of attitudes and institutions.

In the business of nation-building, we must be concerned with effective government exercised with due regard for the kinds of words that are in the Charter. To befriend the *abaissés* is to make human rights operational. In this era of mutual involvement, the simple inescapable basic rule of international law should surely be this: If there are going to be rules, they should be the same rules for all.

The rule of law would mean that spectators of international political Olympiads apply the same criteria of judgment to all—"dispensing a sort of equality to equals and unequals alike," as the Greeks recommended long ago.

Yet in the world today, the spectators of big power politics have a marked tendency to judge each nation by an inequitable standard—its own. A high jumper who has demonstrated his ability to clear seven feet is judged by that measure; other jumpers with less experience and less ambition are regarded as doing very well if they get off the ground at all. The committed nations are to be judged by the degree of their commitment. The uncommitted nations are not to be judged at all, on the ground that they have not agreed to participate in the game.

Even unfair criteria are better, to be sure, than no criteria at all. The very fact that there are rules to be flouted is already evidence of very great progress in human affairs. The battlefield conversion of the troops of Pepin did not usher in the Age of Faith in France—but it was a necessary step along the way. Only a few short years ago, the tenets of liberal democracy that have now become the subject of universal declarations were being repudiated by "civilized" nations whose formidable arms were assigned the task of destroying the cradle of these beliefs.

Nevertheless, there is something grotesque about this double standard when it is applied to real problems in the real world. The Soviets, of all people, are outraged at American support for Cuban refugees. Small nations can vote in the United Nations for world disarmament while wasting resources on the status weapons of modern warfare. High government officials in other continents can be volubly unhappy about the denial of civil rights in the United States, while feeling no special obligation to guarantee human rights to all members of the societies for which they have some immediate responsibility.

The time may well have come to judge the leaders of the uncommitted nations by the standards they apply to others—to judge them not by who they are, but by what they do. It may even be our responsibility to recognize that some peoples are now ready to hear not only of the desire for independence but also of the values of freedom and the importance of government action to guarantee human rights to individuals.

In the post-colonial period the United Nations will have a lot to do with the problem of the nature of government and how these wonderful words that have been put into ratified and unratified conventions can be made to take effect. The time may come when the United Nations' *capacity to befriend* must be linked to its *capacity to act.*

The Capacity to Create

We face a similar problem in the economic challenge of the new nations. The building of institutions in the less developed areas is neither a matter of digging a hole and transplanting Western (whether Russian, European, or American) institutions nor is it a matter of fashioning institutions wholly from local cultural raw materials. It involves a creative synthesis of the two, the development of new institutions that reflect both the cultural and technological necessities of the time and place, modifying the technology to fit the prevailing attitude but also modifying the local culture to make room for the technology.

The development of the *capacity to act* was the first requirement of a collective security organization. The *capacity to befriend* may be next, but the United Nations has demonstrated an allied capacity that may be the most important in the long run—the *capacity to create.* Before a nation can be protected by a classic system of collective security it must in fact become a nation or, at least, it must develop viable economic, social and political institutions. This, in essence, is the goal of the United States foreign aid program and it is the rationale for United Nations technical assistance and pre-investment aid, too.

The creation of these institutions is the most formidable task that organized society has faced since the time of Rome. And it cannot be accomplished simply by transplanting organization and practices from the developed to the underdeveloped states. The fact is that some areas of the world remain without the institutional means of survival in the twentieth century. Here the *capacity to create,* a capacity most effectively exploited by multilateral means, is called for.

The great challenge of multilateral aid is the real foreign aid frontier. Two years ago this writer said as a private citizen that "international affairs for an American in 1959 are primarily the internal affairs of other countries." This statement by itself would seem a heresy in the folklore of diplomacy. Yet, how else to describe foreign aid except as an expression of deep interest in whole development—which includes the "internal affairs"—of another country—for the purpose of enriching that country and at the initiative and with the consent of that country's political authorities.

Herein lies the paradox of foreign aid. Aid given without any conditions or "strings" hardly exists in the real world. If it did it would probably be wasted. Yet the conditions that accompany aid are likely to be resented.

The answer of President Kennedy has been forthright. We have no aid to waste. Furthermore, we will look with regret on the waste of a nation's own sustenance through anachronistic and unjust social policies.

Finally, we are agreed that aid will be dependent upon the existence or creation of programs for institutional, fiscal, agrarian and other reforms when they are needed.

The problem lies in countries which recognize the absence of these preconditions for economic growth—the administrative fibre, the relevant public institutions, the spirit of enterprise, the self-confidence—and need for help in developing them. The new nations of Africa leap to mind, but there are others. Some of these countries are comparatively innocent of the machinery of government. They lack both a literate population or the rudiments of a trained technical and managerial class. Even simple marketing systems are often incomplete or absent.

For such countries the degree of external involvement required to do something large and useful about development is simply massive. Once we accept the need for such involvement by some external group or groups we see clearly both the role and the potential of assistance rendered by the world community at large. Multilateral programs of technical assistance can draw on an international reservoir of bright and inventive technicians and administrators—and can shop around for the best people at the lowest prices. But their most important distinguishing feature is their acceptability in sensitive situations.

Thus a sort of foreign aid spectrum exists. At one end lie the capital projects; at the other end lie the kinds of aid that require long and extensive involvements within a society. It is, of course, quite possible for multilateral assistance to be used along the whole spectrum, and the same is true of bilateral aid. Nevertheless it is often true that on the sensitive end of the spectrum, the work often can only be done by agencies like the World Bank, the United Nations Special Fund or United Nations specialized agencies such as the International Labor Organization, the World Health Organization, the Food and Agricultural Organization, and the United Nations Educational, Scientific and Cultural Organization.

Rapid development in sensitive areas is precisely what now cries for action. There is no question but that the work of international agencies must increase. An example of this can be found in the field of technical assistance. The international agencies have demonstrated their competence and acceptability in technical assistance but there is a great area existing in the world where even technical assistance is too advanced for the situation. The personnel to be assisted are not yet on the job. And even if the organizations were perfect and the necessary personnel in place, we would still lack the ideas. For—let us face it sooner rather than later—our thinkers are still far from having examined systematically, at the level of general theory, the task of nation-building in the less developed world.

The common characteristics of the less developed lands are of course poverty and disorganization. Often described as ultra-nationalist, these countries are usually deficient in nationalism in the meaningful sense of the word. They lack the institutions that permit a citizen to identify his personal interest with those of his fellow-citizens. The problem is one of nation-building.

The importance of institutions familiar to the older nations is easy to demonstrate. The means of transferring them to other countries, the chance of their "taking" in the new host, the thousands of special considerations—about these commonplace mysteries we do not know nearly enough. Economic development seems to be the speciality of every other graduate economist yet the relevant literature on nation-building *as a whole* is thin and still shows too little sign of burgeoning. I am particularly disturbed by the paucity of sound work on the administrative function in economic development and the education of administrators.

It is educational to read in a recent report on education needs in Africa that total disagreement exists on the advisability of a program of large scale primary education. One group thinks it is "almost worse than useless—it creates populations dissatisfied with traditional rural life, aggravates urban social problems, nourishes political turbulence and contributes very little to the economy." On the other hand, according to the report, there are those who argue "that literacy prepares the way for rapid change," the educational program envisaged would call for a tremendous effort on the part of the country involved and substantial assistance from the United States. This seems a question on which scholars might reach for a consensus before precious resources are spent—perhaps only to nourish political turbulence.

As we pointed out in a Maxwell School study published in Syracuse early in 1961, serious research about cross-cultural operations is a very new field of social science endeavor. We have a wealth of evidence from Americans on technical assistance missions, assignments for business firms, and work for mission board and voluntary agencies that the bottleneck in the modernizations process is an institutional one. Absorptive capacity for governmental aid and private investment philanthropy is ultimately measured in every underdeveloped country by the speed at which it can develop the organizations and complex procedures made necessary by modern technology and its attendant division of specialization. Yet we have little systematic understanding about the most relevant and effective ways in which people from one culture participate in building institutions in foreign cultures; the growth of usable theory on this subject has been even slower than the development of applicable theory in the field of economic and industrial development as such.

The accretion of knowledge and the development of wisdom take place in our civilization by the creation of scholarly "literature" on important subjects, so that each person doing scholarly work in the field can stand on the shoulders of others who have worked and published before him. This is the only way modern societies have to avoid repeating again and again the errors which some members of the society have already had the experience to avoid. Syracuse University, together with M.I.T. and too few other universities, are beginning to codify past errors and build the doctrines on which to base future successes. It is still primitive work, but primitive work is the pride of pioneers in every field of intellectual adventure. My complaint would not be the primitive state of research about cross-cultural operations, but the small number of workers in so desperately relevant a vineyard.

The Musts of Parliamentary Diplomacy

We must realize that the United Nations is no longer, either in public discussion or inside the government, a sort of cast-off specialty—subject of concern to a few scholars and to a few specialist tacticians in the government. We must recognize that there is a United Nations angle, presently or prospectively, to every major subject of foreign policy.

We must find means of having the United Nations managed and financed in a way that reflects both the size of the operations and their complexity. The fact that each country has one vote does not mean that each country will pay even .04% of some costs.

We must also realize that when we talk about parliamentary diplomacy or about multilateral operations we are talking about something that is never secret for very long at any stage of the game. In effect we are talking about the diplomacy of public affairs and it is no longer adequate for foreign offices, including the State Department, to think of the public affairs function as primarily a matter of defending yourself against brickbats that are thrown at you for policies after they leak out of somebody else's Foreign Office. In the United Nations the public affairs function has to be half of our diplomacy. In parliamentary diplomacy sometimes the most important channel is the newspapers and the other public media in our communications system.

And finally, in the "must" category, we should not be embarrassed by thinking of the United Nations as an instrument of foreign policy—of American foreign policy; it is also an instrument of everybody else's foreign policy. From our point of view it is not a glittering, sentimental thing we support. It is part of us and it is us, as much as we can make it so. And the fact that it has its own rules, not only of procedure but, in a sense, of ethics, is on the whole useful to us and the restraint that we have to exercise in that ethical frame is a restraint that we welcome.

We cannot afford to mistake parliamentary victories for diplomatic accomplishments. And yet the fact is that the ultimate law of the United Nations is made by its parliament. Whatever is done through the United Nations, indeed whether anything can be done through the United Nations, depends on at least a majority, and on crucial matters, a two-thirds vote in the Assembly. This fact imparts a relevance to leadership in an operational United Nations that can not be ignored. No votes in the United Nations except our own are automatically subject to our interests, but votes will be forthcoming when we lead effectively and in ways that reflect true partnership.

The most important challenge before us is the reaffirmation of our *entente* on the whole subject of the United Nations with the other nations of the Atlantic community. We and they must rebuild a new basis of understanding on our part and on theirs concerning the nature and potential of this evolving institution. We must begin to talk with them about the post-colonial period, and to get their minds and, to some extent, our minds off the present pattern of reacting against the United Nations because it is within the United Nations that the custodians of the 19th-century trading empires are embarrassed—even after they have stopped being colonial powers. We need a reinterpretation of what the Western world can expect from the capacities of the

United Nations and a decision on what we are prepared to do to nurture these capacities. Nothing discussed in this book is as immediate or as important.

The net of all these observations is a controlled optimism in the face of uncontrolled pessimism in certain quarters. The problems this volume looks at in detail are indeed portentous. But the opportunities, for the United Nations and for our relationship with it, are promising and exciting, from the point of view of the values we profess. The very existence of an international organization operating through parliamentary and democratic forms is a projection onto the world scene of the concept of an open society.

7

UNITED STATES POLICY IN THE UNITED NATIONS

by

FRANCIS O. WILCOX*

IT HAS BEEN said that if the United Nations were not in existence it would have to be invented. This is something that many of us tend to forget in the United States where we are inclined to evaluate political institutions in terms of short-range successes or failures rather than the longer-range goals to which they are dedicated. It is a mistake which we can not afford to make about the United Nations. Its goals are so important that, in spite of temporary disappointments or set-backs, we must continue to help make it an effective instrumentality for world peace.

The Present Status of the United Nations

No one can deny that we are facing a very critical period in

* Adapted from an address before the American Academy of Political and Social Science which appeared in the *Annals* of the Academy in July, 1961.

the history of the United Nations. Some people go so far as to predict that the United Nations is already doomed to suffer the fate of the League of Nations. I am not that pessimistic. Nevertheless, the extremely difficult situation that confronts the United Nations in the Congo, the persistent attacks of the Soviet Union upon the Secretary General, the serious financial crisis that afflicts the Organization, together with the negative attitude that General de Gaulle has recently expressed—these things suggest that it is really in a period of grave jeopardy.

Among American supporters of the United Nations there are still other causes for serious concern. The principal one stems from the view that the substantial majority which the United States has enjoyed in the General Assembly from the beginning is apparently being whittled away by the influx of new members and the more aggressive attitude of the Soviet Union and its satellite states.

With respect to the future, there are many uncertain elements in the picture. It is somewhat early to make any long-range predictions about the future of the United Nations or our relationship to it. It is clear, however, that one very important element in the situation remains the attitude of the small states, both old and new. It is not yet clear whether our friends will act with the degree of unity and solidarity that is necessary; nor is it clear that the new members of the Organization will act with the responsibility which the situation requires.

Another uncertain element is the Soviet attitude. Soviet tactics in the United Nations will, no doubt, reflect the state of our bilateral relationships with the Soviet Union. Just what their posture will be will depend, in part at least, upon the soundings which they are conducting with respect to the Kennedy Administration.

Mr. Khrushchev's Proposal

Let us go back to the Fifteenth General Assembly, when the present crisis began with Mr. Khrushchev's appearance in New York. It is true that he received a great deal of publicity throughout the country. I do not believe, however, that he achieved his objectives. Certainly he did not have his way about the Congo. He did not destroy the United Nations. He did not get to debate the question of disarmament in the Assembly as he wanted to do. Moreover, his incredibly bad manners—exhibited when he pounded the desk with his shoe, when he called the Security Council a spittoon, and when he referred to the Philippine delegate as a stooge and a jerk—shocked many delegates who obviously had higher regard for dignified parliamentary behavior than Mr. Khrushchev did.

Far more dangerous to the United Nations was his proposal that Mr. Hammarskjold resign and be replaced with three Secretaries General, each armed with a veto power. There has been a good deal of speculation as to just what Mr. Khrushchev had in mind when he launched his bitter attack upon the Secretary General. Was he attempting to destroy the Organization? Was he bent on eliminating the Secretary General, who has given more direction and purpose to the United Nations than Mr. Khrushchev thought desirable? Was he subjecting the world to cold war tactics on the ground it is good psychology to stir up trouble now and then? Or was he putting on an act to convince the Red Chinese that he is a tough leader who can command attention outside the communist sphere?

Students of Soviet history may recall the words Lenin wrote forty years ago when he reminded the Bolsheviks they were "obliged to carry on the struggle in parliament in order to destroy parliament." Perhaps that is what Mr. Khrushchev had in mind. One can only speculate about his objectives. The fact is, however, that if his proposal to create three Secretaries General were adopted, it would be an irreparable blow to the United Nations. It would water down the Secretariat to the point where it would have no vitality and would threaten it with a veto on every important issue. One can imagine what would happen if Mr. Hammarskjold had to secure the countersignatures of two colleagues, one from the Communist world and one from the so-called neutralist world, every time he sent a telegram of instructions to the Congo!

During the past fifteen years, we have learned how much a competent Secretariat made up of fair minded, intelligent individuals can do on behalf of peace. It would be a tragic thing if that lesson were now forgotten or discarded. I do not believe it will be. Indeed, many people realize that Mr. Khrushchev's attack upon the United Nations is not only a danger; it is, in its way, a compliment to the Organization. The fact is the United Nations has proved an effective obstacle to the very thing that seems to interest the Soviet Union most at this time in history; that is, destroying the independence and integrity of small countries. In any event, the extreme proposal Mr. Khrushchev made had practically no support outside the Soviet bloc.

The Possibility of Compromise

One of the dangers we now face lies in further ill-conceived moves to compromise with the Soviet Union. All too often the Soviet Union has made an outrageous proposal with the expectation that other member countries will take up the cudgel on behalf of a second proposal perhaps only a half or a third as outrageous as the original. In this way a spirit of compromise is generated which can lead to harmful results unless it is properly checked. A great majority of the members, I think, understand Mr. Khrushchev's proposal for just what it was—an attack, not upon the United States, or on Mr. Hammarskjold as a person, or on what he is doing in the Congo, but upon the United Nations itself. Recognizing this, they have rallied to the support of an effective United Nations and an effective Secretary General.

To the smaller nations, the United Nations has enormous value. It was designed to protect their independence and their integrity and to help them in advancing their people's welfare. It is also a center where a small state can greatly enhance its influence by joining with other like-minded states to achieve common objectives. But most important, membership in the United Nations is a symbol of each country's standing and dignity as a sovereign state. In the circumstances one can understand why many of these countries resented Mr. Khrushchev's proposal.

Representation for Asia and Africa

I agree with the Soviet contention that the United Nations should be reorganized so as to reflect the realities of the 1960's. But what is needed is not a reshuffling of the Secretariat. What is needed is an increase in the seats available in the Security Council and the Economic and Social Council so as to give adequate representation to the countries of Asia and Africa. Although the membership of the United Nations has nearly doubled in fifteen years, during that time the size of the major councils has remained exactly the same.

The Security Council, for example, was set up as a body of eleven members designed to represent the interests of 51 countries. Since San Francisco, however, 48 members have been added to the United Nations, many of which aspire to membership on the Council. Since most of the new members come from Asia and Africa, it follows that these are the areas that are most drastically underrepresented. But these countries are deeply interested in the United Nations. They come to the Organization with new ideas and enthusiasm, and we must use this creative energy by providing ample opportunities for them to participate in its activities. The latest addition of seventeen members makes any further delay both undesirable and intolerable.

Now, you may ask, why has not this been done? For the simple reason that the Soviet Union made it clear that it would not permit any amendments to the Charter unless Red China were admitted. The Soviet delegate made this very emphatic when he repeated his point in Russian, English, French, Spanish, and Chinese so that no one could possibly misunderstand.

This leads me to make one comment about the role of the smaller states in the United Nations. They carry a tremendous responsibility for, to a great extent, the future and the destiny of the Organization lies in their hands. If they play their role with courage and conviction, and if they will stand up for what is right, they can do much to assure for the United Nations a reasonably bright future. But if they are weak and irresolute, if they are divided and uncertain, they will lose a great opportunity to promote the cause of world peace. There is a real challenge here for the small states who can, if they will, encourage the Soviet Union to move to a more reasonable course of action through the inexorable force of public opinion. I am not suggesting that they support the United States in all respects; all I am asking is that they give their loyal support to the United Nations and the principles for which it stands.

Soviet Imperialism

In this connection, a word should be said about Soviet imperialism. Everywhere in Asia and Africa during the last fifteen years, new countries have come of age and have been granted their freedom. Over a billion people have earned the right to govern themselves and have become members of the United Nations. The Western colonial systems have rapidly liquidated themselves, leaving behind a framework of modern techniques and aspirations. On the whole, this process has been remarkably peaceful. There has been some turmoil, to be sure. But, in general, states have won their independence by peaceful means, by the vote, by passive resistance, and by demonstrating their capacity to handle their own affairs.

As this process has altered the face of the globe, the direct opposite was taking place all around the Soviet periphery. Wherever the influence of the Red Army could be brought to bear, independent countries were being snuffed out or reduced to puppet status. Except where the free world made it clear that Soviet force would not be permitted to prevail, every state bordering on the Soviet Union lost its independence.

Here is one of the most striking paradoxes of our time. The Soviet Union seeks to pose as the champion of oppressed peoples. But clearly the Soviet Union and Red China are the only important imperialist powers left today. In October 1960, while we were debating colonialism in the Assembly, I was reminding the delegations present of this fact when I was interrupted by violent outbursts from the Rumanian delegation and by vigorous shoe pounding on the part of Mr. Khrushchev. This rude and intemperate behavior, which certainly shocked most delegates, is a clear indication that the Soviet satellite system is the tenderest spot in the Soviet anatomy.

It is obvious from this and other examples, that what the Soviet Union wants is a double standard in the United Nations. They want to feel perfectly free to criticize other countries for their shortcomings, but they cannot bear to have anyone tell the truth about their own misdeeds. So far as the United States is concerned, I hope we will continue to tell the truth about Soviet colonialism. And if the shoe fits, then the Soviet delegate ought to put it on, rather than pound the table with it.

Soviet Attitude Towards the UN

In our attempt to understand the attitude of the Soviet Union towards the United Nations, it is important to recall one of the basic truths which govern the participation of *any* nation in an international organization: a state ordinarily decides to participate as a means of furthering its own national objectives. In the United Nations there are many countries whose long-range goals coincide with those of the Charter. The United States is one of these countries. There are others whose policy objectives appear to be at variance with the principles of the United Nations but who have joined the Organization because they hope to utilize it to serve their own purposes. The Soviet Union falls into the latter category.

The Charter dedicates the United Nations to the maintenance of peace; to the development of friendly relations between nations; and to cooperation in the solution of the major problems which beset mankind. Simply stated, the goal of the United Nations is to help create those conditions which will make it possible for man, living in peace with his neighbors, to enjoy material and spiritual growth. The United States does not have any reluctance in sincerely subscribing to goals like these. Our national aims and the aims of the United Nations are basically the same.

The Soviet Union, on the other hand, has often proclaimed its determination to win the world to communism. It has pursued this aim through overt aggression, economic imperialism, subversion, and threat of force. To the Soviet Union, membership does not mean adherence to United Nations objectives, except insofar as Soviet leaders judge that these can be used to advance the interests of the Soviet Union and world communism. It is a marriage of convenience and not of love.

We are frequently reminded that, as a member of the League of Nations, the Soviet Union championed the principle of collective security and the idea of universal disarmament. On the whole their operating strategy was one of political expediency. When their security was threatened by the aggressive designs of fascism and national socialism they supported the League with enthusiasm. When, on the other hand, the League tended to clash with Soviet objectives they flouted its authority the moment it suited their purposes.

Just what Soviet leaders had in mind when they joined the United Nations is not clear. It may be, as some believe, they were motivated primarily by considerations of national security or by the pressure of world opinion. It may be they regarded the United Nations as a counter-revolutionary bourgeois parliament which they joined to undermine and destroy from within. Or it may be they had no preconceived notions about their relations with the Organization, but joined with the idea of cooperating or not as their national interests dictate from time to time.

Whatever theory one may hold, it is apparent that the Soviet attitude towards the United Nations is not static; it is evolving with the changing world scene. It is equally apparent that Soviet leaders, despite their frequent expressions of contempt and disdain, view participation in the United Nations as an important aspect of their policy.

There are a good many reasons why this is so. By maintaining membership in the United Nations, Soviet leaders can promote the idea of their own respectability and humanitarianism, qualities notably lacking in the Soviet approach. Moreover, they can utilize the great world forum to spread to an increasingly wide audience, the communist recipe for peace. Above all, they can seek to frustrate, or at least blunt, from within the Organization, any contemplated action which might conflict with the communist program.

From the Soviet point of view this requires a greater degree of control over the United Nations than they have been able to exercise during the past 15 years. Now they are doing their utmost to make up for lost time. In addition to their attack upon the Secretary General, they have attempted to extend their influence in a variety of ways:

1. They insisted upon parity in the disarmament negotiations thus winning equal representation (a five-to-five ratio) for Soviet bloc and Western countries. This victory they are now using as a precedent in their constant attempt to gain status and prestige for their satellite states in United Nations circles.

2. They have refused to pay their share of the cost of the United Nations Emergency Force in the Middle East and of the Congo operation in spite of the fact that these costs were

approved by the Assembly, in accordance with the provisions of the Charter. Thus they are attempting to extend their veto power to the General Assembly.

3. They have demanded of the Secretary General that at least 50 Soviet citizens be placed in key posts in the United Nations Secretariat. Since the Soviets reject the principle of an objective international civil service, these additions would permit them to slant the policies and programs of the United Nations in the direction of communism.

4. They have done an about face and renewed their interest in the specialized agencies whose programs of social and economic betterment they used to regard with utter contempt. This was done to win the support of the underdeveloped countries.

5. They have greatly intensified their efforts to win, for themselves and their satellites, committee chairmanships and other posts of influence and prestige in the United Nations.

6. Finally, it is well known that in their relations with other delegations they are following more flexible tactics than in the past. On occasion they have even switched from their traditional hard line to a friendly and co-operative approach.

Clearly no one of these steps, looked at alone, would constitute a serious threat to the integrity of the United Nations. But taken together they indicate the important dimensions of the offensive mounted by the Soviet Union. How far will this offensive go? No one can predict with any degree of accuracy. We know from bitter experience, however, that whenever Soviet leaders get their foot in a door they do not take it out unless someone steps on their corns.

At the present writing, the Soviet "troika" policy is spreading like poison ivy. In Geneva the Soviet delegation recently demanded that the control organ contemplated for the nuclear test-ban treaty be headed up by an East-West-Neutral bloc triumvirate with a built-in veto. A somewhat similar demand has been made with respect to the international control commission on Laos. And if press reports are accurate, comparable demands will be put forth in connection with any future disarmament negotiations.

This is the veto principle in a new and expanded form. In effect Soviet leaders are saying that in the future they do not intend to subject the Soviet Union to any joint action which affects the vital interests of their country unless they have the right to cast the deciding vote. If this position is held, it will not only make serious negotiations between the communist bloc and the West practically impossible; it will do irreparable damage to the whole fabric of international relations that has been laboriously built up since the turn of the century.

Suggestions of a Procedural or Organizational Nature

With this background in mind, let us turn to a few suggestions relating to the strengthening of the United Nations and the improvement of our position in it. I do this with some temerity, because different people draw different conclusions from the same experience; what I have learned during the past fifteen years might not coincide with what others have learned.

Unity Among the Free Countries

From an organizational and procedural point of view, it is of the utmost importance that we strongly encourage a greater spirit of unity and teamwork among free nations in the Organization. True, the United States does not want satellites and we certainly want to avoid leaving the impression that we are trying to create a *bloc* of states within the United Nations. We have always been proud of the strength that comes from diversity of view and independence of action. Nevertheless, as the Soviet Union intensifies its efforts in the United Nations to subvert, to disrupt, to discredit, and to destroy, the free nations will have to accept that challenge for what it is worth. They will find it necessary to concert on their policies and programs and coordinate their activities far more than they have in the past if they are to preserve the integrity of the United Nations and move ahead with the objectives of the free world.

At present one of the weakest links in the free world chain stems from the coolness of France. Incensed by the Suez incident, and angered by the repeated needling they regularly receive from the Assembly on Algeria, the French have been somewhat less than enthusiastic about the Organization during the past few years. On occasion this aloofness seriously handicaps the efforts of the free nations to take vigorous and constructive action.

Today, however, Suez is five years behind us, and the problem of Algeria is hopefully on its way towards solution. Even more pertinent is the fact that many French-speaking members of the French community, who entered the United Nations in 1960, look to the Quai d'Orsay for guidance and counsel. Many friends of France hope the French will soon turn another page and begin to play once more the helpful and influential role they are capable of playing.

This leads me to comment briefly on the attitude of Western Europe generally. I have talked to many diplomats from the area during the past few years and, as a rule, they are quite pessimistic about the United Nations. As one Foreign Minister put it: "The Assembly is becoming increasingly unwieldy and unreliable as a result of the influx of new members from Asia and Africa. Given the anti-colonial sentiment that exists there, the cards are stacked against the countries of Western Europe; we do not think we can take any important issue to the UN and hope to get a fair deal. We do not intend to withdraw, but as the United Nations is presently constituted it is certainly not something we can rely on to protect our national interests."

One can appreciate the growing concern which these countries have. At the same time it can be argued that the United Nations holds very important benefits for them which they should not underestimate. It is, for example, by far the most powerful force in the world today working to give validity to those rules of conduct in international relations which the West has traditionally stood for. Still more important, the United Nations offers the only viable alternative to the old colonial system, providing, as it does, opportunities for peaceful adjustment and continued cooperation in the working relations between newly-emerging states and the former mother countries.

Dutch New Guinea (or West Irian) and Angola might be cited as cases in point. Obviously, new relationships between these areas, on the one hand, and the Netherlands and Portugal on the other, will have to be evolved. The United Nations, if it is given a chance, can help find these relationships. To paraphrase a distinguished poet, we are in fact "wandering between two worlds, one dead, the other powerless to be born." In this situation, which is of the utmost political and economic importance to many of the countries of Western Europe, the United Nations can serve as an indispensable midwife.

I come back to my emphasis upon the need for greater unity and teamwork among the free nations. The fact is, the growth of communist power and influence in the United Nations is going to compel the free countries, sooner or later, to work much more closely together than they have in the past, and the sooner this is done the less painful it will be.

Senor de Madariaga, the Spanish statesman and author, put it well when he wrote:

"The trouble today is that the Communist world understands unity but not liberty, while the free world understands liberty but not unity. Eventual victory may be won by the first of the the two sides to achieve the synthesis of both liberty and unity."

The General Assembly: Some Procedural Needs

The time has come also for us to urge a thorough review of the organization and procedures of the Assembly. The sheer size of the United Nations—if last year is any indication of the problems involved—makes such a review imperative. Otherwise the Assembly may degenerate into an unwieldy propaganda forum incapable of taking effective action. Bolivia, Costa Rica, and the United Kingdom proposed last year that a study be made of Assembly procedures with the idea of making it a more effective instrumentality for world peace. This is definitely in the interests of the United Nations and the free world, and we should strongly support such a move.

Are other organs of the United Nations—such as the Security Council, the Economic and Social Council, the International Court of Justice, and the Secretariat—being used to the best possible advantage? Could the Assembly devolve more of its task upon subsidiary organs which could function between sessions of the Assembly? Can more satisfactory methods be devised to insure the selection of competent presiding officers and other officials? Would a system of subcommittees be helpful in easing the work-load of the seven regular committees of the Assembly? Is there any acceptable way of effectively limiting debate in the Assembly? Can more adequate methods be agreed upon for screening the items to be included on the agenda? What can be done to clarify the rules of procedure, some of which have been subject to serious abuse in recent years?

These are only a few of the questions which ought to be examined in connection with any attempt to review the organization and procedures of the Assembly. They indicate, however, how important the task is.

In that connection, I was interested to note in 1960 the extent to which the Soviet bloc has developed its working knowledge of parliamentary tactics and procedures. In the early days most of the able parliamentarians came from Western Europe, Latin America, and the Old Commonwealth countries. This is no longer true. Today the Soviet bloc, and certain Afro-Asian delegates, are becoming more skilled in parliamentary tactics, and in some cases they have used this skill to good advantage. During the last Assembly there seemed to be a dearth of able, free-world delegates who knew the practices and procedures of the Assembly and who were willing to assume leadership roles. If this is a trend it certainly ought to be reversed.

United States Delegation in New York

Now let us turn briefly to the representation of the United States in the United Nations. In addition to strengthening our mission in New York—which has already been done—one improvement which occurs to me immediately has to do with the nature of the delegation which we send to the Assembly. I think the time has come when we should move in the direction of professionalizing our delegation. There can be no doubt that outstanding Americans have made remarkable contributions to our work in the United Nations both during their service on the delegation and after returning to their local communities. Today, however, in view of the fact that the United Nations is a much more complex operation than it used to be, and in view of the fact that the Soviet Union is taking a more aggressive attitude, we should utilize to the fullest the talents of our skilled diplomats at the ambassadorial level. The stakes are too high to do otherwise. Certainly it is unfair for our government to expect newcomers to diplomacy to compete on even terms with Deputy Foreign Ministers from Moscow and Soviet Ambassadors to London, Paris, and Rome who have attended many meetings of the Assembly. If outsiders are used as delegates, then our government should consider inviting individuals who have served on previous delegations or who have had comparable diplomatic experience.

In that connection, there is much that can be done to improve our representation procedures. We have been short of representation funds, and we have not had satisfactory housing arrangements for personnel living in New York. We must never lose sight of the fact that there are now ninety-nine members instead of fifty-one, and the task of explaining our point of view and of winning support for our policies will be much greater than it used to be. It is no longer sufficient to maintain close working relations with a relatively few key delegations; we must strive to establish wider and more systematic contacts with many delegations. It is true that good will cannot be bought at the dinner table, but neither should our mission in New York be handicapped by a shortage of entertainment funds.

In that connection, too, it is obvious that we ought to do what we can, on an urgent basis, to encourage hospitable treatment for United Nations delegations from the new countries of Asia and Africa. One person turned away from an eating establishment because of the color of his skin can do much to offset the good will laboriously built up over months of time. The citizens of New York—as well as our United States Mission there—are doing noble work in extending hospitality and in easing problems relating to such matters as housing and educational facilities for newly arrived diplomats and their families. It is time the American people in every state realized that what they do as individuals—in the field of race relations especially—can have an important bearing upon the achievement of our national objectives in the United Nations.

US Attitude Towards Substantive Issues

I have outlined some of the procedural and organizational problems that need attention. Progress in these directions can contribute materially towards the improvement of our posture in the United Nations. Far more important, however, are substantive issues on which, for a variety of reasons, our government has taken what many other countries consider an essentially negative stand. Whether we will wish to make further adjustments in our policies I do not know, but clearly we could improve our position if we could relax somewhat our attitude towards these problems.

Admission of Red China

First and foremost is the problem of Red China. Many people argue vigorously that, at long last, we should face up to reality and agree to the seating of Communist China before we are pushed into an ignominious surrender on communist terms. It is true that in 1960 our delegation carried our position in the Assembly only after hard work to line up support, and then only by a narrow voting margin. It is true, also, that a good many friendly states vote with us not because they share our convictions but only because we ask them to. Moreover, if the attitudes expressed recently in Brazil, Canada, and the United Kingdom are indicative of the shifting tide of world opinion, it is probably true that the moratorium formula—whereby the Assembly decides to postpone for another year further discussion of the China problem—may have outlived its usefulness.

There are two factors, however, that would make any satisfactory solution of the China question extremely difficult at this time. The first is the strong opposition of the American people and of the Congress to the seating of Red China. This opposition was vigorously reflected in both party platforms in 1960 and in the campaign speeches of Mr. Nixon and Mr. Kennedy. It was reiterated in May, 1961, during Vice-President Lyndon Johnson's visit to Asia. If popular support for the United Nations in this country were to fall away as a result of the admission of Red China, this would, indeed, be a very serious handicap for the future of the Organization.

The second factor is the discouragingly negative attitude of both Nationalist and Red China—the latter being particularly vocal in its negativism. So long as these governments refuse to talk about the possibility of any solution that would envisage the presence of the other China in the Organization, the United States would find it difficult to move off dead center. This is especially true in view of our mutual defense treaty with Nationalist China and our obligations to help preserve the integrity of Taiwan as an independent entity.

In this evolving situation, it would seem to me that our government might well take as its point of departure the continuing membership of Nationalist China. It is my impression that relatively few states would wish to support a solution which would result in forcing Nationalist China out of the United Nations; many of them may be sincere in their desire to have Communist China in, but it does not follow that they want Nationalist China out. If a separate vote could be taken on this issue alone, I believe that a substantial majority would be recorded against extinction of Taiwan as an independent state.

This being the case—if the moratorium formula should prove no longer workable—we should look towards the formulation of a new tactial position in the United Nations which would tap this attitude of mind. If this were done we would, in effect, be taking steps to shift the onus for the failure to seat Red China to the Peiping government where it belongs; first, because it has not behaved like a government ought to behave in order to be welcomed into the United Nations; and second, because it continues vigorously to oppose what other members believe to be a reasonable solution to the problem.

It will be argued that this suggestion is only a temporary expedient that fails to get at the basic issue involved in the Red China question. As a next step, however, it would put us in a more positive posture than we have maintained during recent years.

United Nations Economic Assistance

A second area where we have taken a somewhat negative position has to do with the extension of aid to underdeveloped areas. For some years, many members have loudly insisted that the United States ought to take the lead in setting up a large-scale economic development program under the auspices of the United Nations. If there is any one thing the underdeveloped areas want, it is the kind of development program in which they can sit down around a table with their colleagues in order to discuss and plan, on the basis of equality, the economic development of their countries.

There are two principal arguments one often hears against our participation in this kind of program. The first is that it would cost too much. If we were to get involved in this type of activity, the argument runs, it would soon develop into a bottomless pit into which we might be called upon to pour out countless billions of dollars in the almost hopeless task of raising to a reasonable level the standard of living of the rest of the world. The fact is, of course, there exists in United Nations procedures a built-in control which automatically regulates the contribution the United States would have to make to any program of this nature; that is the ability of *other* countries to contribute their fair share. It is easier for us to meet our financial obligations in the United Nations than it is for most other members of the Organization to meet theirs. So in the normal process of drawing up an acceptable contributions scale, there is a built-in thermostat that would keep the expenditures of the United Nations within reasonable bounds.

The other argument has to do with the role of the Soviet Union and the possibility that any such development program might fall under Russian domination or Russian control. I believe this is a misleading argument which we ought to look at again in the light of our experience in the Organization. During the past fifteen years we have participated in many United Nations activities which have required special financing —including the Children's Fund, the Technical Assistance Program, the Special Fund, and several refugee programs—and in none of these has the Soviet Union exercised undue influence. I doubt that the threat of Soviet control would be serious in connection with economic development, particularly since the Soviet Union has not shown the slightest interest in making a contribution to such a program.

We would certainly want to avoid imposing upon the United Nations a larger program than it could digest effectively. We might, therefore, develop a formula which would permit us to divert aid funds from bilateral to multilateral channels gradually over a period of time as the United Nations proves its worth. This would have the double advantage of strengthening the United Nations and of producing at least twice as much aid per dollar as is now furnished by our bilateral assistance programs. It would also win for the United States an incalculable amount of good will.

Colonial Questions

Still a third area where the United States has often taken a relatively negative position lies in the ill-defined field of colonialism. Many of our friends cannot understand why we talk so much about freedom and independence and then support our NATO partners on concrete colonial issues. In recent years it has been clear to many of us why our government has not always been able to vote with the Asian and African countries on colonial questions. In many instances we have been deeply torn between our NATO alliance, on the one hand, and our sympathy with the aspirations of the newly developing countries on the other. In view of the importance of our security ties with Western Europe we have hesitated to vote for any proposal that might have the effect of weakening the NATO system.

But what was true a few years ago does not necessarily remain true today. At this period in history the process of liquidating the colonial empires of the Western nations has reached such an advanced stage that few occasions will arise in the future when a specific vote by the United States will result in a weakening of the NATO alliance. It seems to me, therefore, that we are in a fairly good position to encourage our Western allies to move ahead with the final steps of the liquidation process. At the same time we ought to make it clear to them that they should not expect us to support their position on colonial questions—merely because of our alliance—where the bitter opposition of the Asian-African countries is certain to result.

Such a policy would inevitably bring in its wake angry charges that the United States is deserting its NATO partners to curry favor with its African friends. This is precisely what happened when we voted for a United Nations inquiry into Portugal's policy in Angola. On the horns of this dilemma our government has a two-fold task to perform; that of reassuring Western Europe and at the same time convincing Africa (and Asia) that the strengthening of NATO is not at all inconsistent with the development of peace and progress in Africa.

Indeed, from our point of view the two things are quite complementary. For unless Western Europe continues to prosper, there will not be sufficient financial and human resources to make real headway in the development of the African continent. If our African friends understood this basic principle more thoroughly, they might be somewhat less reluctant, in the United Nations, in compelling us to choose between support for our NATO alliance and support for Africa.

Other Issues: The Financial Crisis

Space will not permit detailed discussion of other issues. Clearly, however, the extent to which the United States can improve its posture in the United Nations with respect to such matters as disarmament, Palestine refugees, human rights, and the Congo will depend upon a number of factors closely bound up with our total foreign policy objectives. It is desirable, of course, to be on the winning side of votes in the Assembly, but friendly relations in the United Nations is not an end in itself. We do not want to get involved in a popularity contest, particularly if our over-all foreign policy goals should suffer in the process.

With respect to the Congo, it is a source of some satisfaction to me that our government has given its unflagging support to the United Nations in its efforts to bring stability to that unhappy land. The situation there is still bad enough, but if it had not been for our consistent help the United Nations would have failed in its mission, and utter chaos would have descended upon the Congo.

Meanwhile, the Congo situation underscores the precarious financial predicament of the Organization. Somehow a method must be found to provide a more substantial and a more reliable fiscal base for the United Nations. It is a terrible thing to have the Secretary General go around with his hat in his hand desperately trying to collect enough money to take care of world crises that arise.

In some ways the financial crisis the United Nations is trying to surmount constitutes a greater threat to the integrity of the Organization than the excessive use of the veto. It is obvious that unless the members rally to the support of the United Nations its future usefulness will be seriously limited and it will run the grave risk of foundering on the shoals of fiscal insolvency.

The greatest single obstacle to financial stability lies in the categorical refusal of the Soviet Union to contribute its share of the expenses of the Congo operation on the ground that it does not approve what the United Nations is doing there. But is this a sound basis for any nation to refuse to contribute? Is it not obvious that if every member were free to pick and choose the portions of the Organization's budget it is willing to help finance that we would have fiscal chaos?

This is precisely the reason the Charter imposes on all members the obligation to pay their share of expenses as apportioned by the General Assembly. It is the reason, also, that any member whose arrears equal the amount of contributions due for the preceding two years must forfeit its voting rights.

Even if the added expense imposed by the Congo should double the budget, the cost of supporting the United Nations is still incredibly small. In 1959, our contribution to all United Nations activities amounted to only sixty-one cents per capita. With United Nations expenditures then running something over $200,000,000 per year, and world arms expenditures running nearly $125 billion, it is obvious that the nations of the world have not yet put the Organization in proper perspective. We have not yet attached to it the significance it deserves in its all-important task of keeping the peace.

As the Secretary-General has stated, the United Nations has two alternatives: it must face the economic consequences of its own actions, or it must change the substantive policies on which those actions are based. The time has come for the United States to take the lead in seeking new sources of revenue for the Organization. Perhaps consultant fees could be charged member governments for services rendered in connection with technical assistance and economic development activities. Or, better yet as a source of revenue, small fees might be collected for the United Nations on the issuance of passports or visas, on waterway tolls, or on mail going across national boundary lines. Such suggestions will, of course, meet with strong opposition on the part of those who are fearful of endowing the Organization with powers of a supra-national character; but unless member states begin to demonstrate a greater sense of fiscal responsibility than most of them have shown up to the present time, some drastic steps will have to be taken if the United Nations is to discharge its responsibilities in the difficult period ahead.

Basically, of course, the problem is more political than financial. So long as some countries cannot agree that activities such as those in the Gaza strip and the Congo are vital to the maintenance of peace, then we can expect recurring financial crises in the United Nations as bitter symptoms of the disease of mistrust and suspicion that still plagues the world.

Concluding Comment

The United States should continue to do what it can to improve its posture in the United Nations and to strengthen that Organization. The sad fact remains, however, that Soviet leaders are not interested in making the United Nations effective. They believe that a strong United Nations works against their interests and their determination to create a communist world. They want to be free to foment turmoil and confusion in various parts of the world without the restraining influence of an effective international organization.

At San Francisco the United Nations was built upon the assumption that the cooperation of the great powers which had worked together to win the war would continue in their joint efforts to keep the peace. Yet in the fifteen years that I have followed the activities of the Organization, I cannot recall a single instance when the Soviet Union enthusiastically supported one move to make the United Nations a stronger, more effective agency for world peace.

We have learned, over the years, that peace cannot be ushered in by a Charter, no matter how well conceived or how well drafted. But the choice before us, I think, is quite clear. Either we continue to move ahead with the United Nations toward a regime of order and stability under world law, or we begin to fall back down that slippery slope towards the point of no return where every state works solely for itself, and brute force is the final arbiter.

This somber fact confronts the smaller states particularly with a very grave challenge. It can be argued—although I think not too convincingly—that the United States could get along without the United Nations. At least we are strong enough to stand on our own feet and defend ourselves. Certainly this is not true of the smaller nations. They need the protective umbrella of the United Nations—and the code of ethics which it encourages—for the preservation of their existence as independent states.

Peace with justice is the most important goal to which we can aspire. On that most of us can agree. But peace must have adequate foundations if it is to endure. One of these foundations is that nations must live by the principles of international law and order. Another is that they must settle their disputes by peaceful means. Still a third is the active awareness that human beings are entitled to more than mere subsistence.

The United Nations provides the main instrument available to the world for the attainment of these essentials of peace. It may not be perfect but it is the best the wit of man has been able to devise.

Of one thing I am certain: it is essential that we and the other free members of the United Nations never give up our quest for a just and lasting peace. We must never give in to despair; we must never permit ourselves to become fatalistic about the prospects of a nuclear war. Thucydides reminds us that fatalism tends to produce what it dreads, for men do not oppose that which they consider inevitable.

It follows that the smaller states have a great responsibility to give the United Nations the loyal support it needs to proceed with its task. This is, indeed, a case of mutual survival. If the smaller states will rise to the occasion and help make the United Nations a truly effective organization, we stand a good chance of having some semblance of peace in our lifetime.

INDEX

D

E

F

L

M

N

T

U

V

W

Y